T0356642

Plan Your Prosperity

Fisher Investments Press

Fisher Investments Press brings the research, analysis, and market intelligence of Fisher Investments' research team, headed by founder, Executive Chairman, and *New York Times* best-selling author Ken Fisher, to all investors. The Press covers a range of investing and market-related topics for a wide audience—from novices to enthusiasts to professionals.

Books by Ken Fisher

Markets Never Forget (But People Do)
Debunkery
How to Smell a Rat
The Ten Roads to Riches
The Only Three Questions That Still Count
100 Minds That Made the Market
The Wall Street Waltz
Super Stocks

Fisher Investments Series

Own the World by Aaron Anderson
20/20 Money by Michael Hanson

Fisher Investments On Series

Fisher Investments on Consumer Discretionary
Fisher Investments on Consumer Staples
Fisher Investments on Emerging Markets
Fisher Investments on Energy
Fisher Investments on Financials
Fisher Investments on Health Care
Fisher Investments on Industrials
Fisher Investments on Materials
Fisher Investments on Technology
Fisher Investments on Telecom
Fisher Investments on Utilities

FISHER
INVESTMENTS
PRESS

Plan Your Prosperity

THE ONLY RETIREMENT GUIDE YOU'LL EVER NEED, STARTING NOW—WHETHER YOU'RE 22, 52, OR 82

Second Edition

Ken Fisher
with Lara Hoffmans and Chris Ciarmiello

WILEY

Published by John Wiley & Sons, Inc., Hoboken, New Jersey.
Published simultaneously in Canada.

For general information on our other products and services or for technical support, please contact our Customer Care Department within the United States at (800) 762-2974, outside the United States at (317) 572-3993 or fax (317) 572-4002.

Wiley also publishes its books in a variety of electronic formats. Some content that appears in print may not be available in electronic formats. For more information about Wiley products, visit our web site at www.wiley.com.

Library of Congress Cataloging-in-Publication Data is Available:

ISBN 9781394318841 (Cloth)
ISBN 9781394318889 (ePub)
ISBN 9781394318872 (ePDF)

Cover Design: Paul McCarthy
Cover Art: © Getty Images | Chris Clor

SKY10099585_030725

Contents

Contents

Preface

So much investing commentary and so many books talk about tactics: how to find winning stocks, how to avoid the next great crash, how to time cryptocurrency booms, how to know whether value or growth or tech or renewable energy stocks will reign, how to pick the right tools to use, and how to use methods the author favors. Or they cover market forecasting—as most of my 11 books do.

This one is different.

When I first wrote this book in 2012, many investors—still stung by 2008's massive bear market—could see no path to retirement. They were lost at sea without a plan, compass, map, or lighthouse to help guide them through the inherently uncertain and long journey retirement investing always is. Tactics are one thing. But before tactics make any sense, one has to decide on the real keys to any long-term plan.

Your goals. Your time horizon (the length of time your assets need to work to achieve those goals). Your comfort with volatility. All this culminates in an asset allocation—the mix of stocks, bonds, cash, and other securities that deliver a likely path to attaining your goals. And the selection of a benchmark that fits with this.

These are fundamental and timeless aspects of my investment process that never change. They are the lighthouse on the far side of the waterway. They are something every investor should have—and should check back to in times of turmoil. Yet far too many don't. That is where this book comes in. Its purpose, then as now, is to help you think through those factors. To help you build your own lighthouse.

Wall Street doesn't help much—often drawing false distinctions between financial planning and retirement planning, hyping retirement as a fundamental investment strategy game changer. Much of this talk and the associated planning are little more than fancied-up sales pitches. This book isn't here to sell you anything. It is designed to help clarify how you think about retirement investing.

What's new here, anyway?

This second edition doesn't change any of that. But in the years since I wrote the first edition, I found a few things potentially wanting in it. First, while I still think financial planning is too often a Trojan horse for sales pitches, it is apparent many people need help with things like tax and insurance planning and, as it specifically pertains to this book, retirement withdrawal planning. This second edition fills that gap with an all-new appendix.

Furthermore, in the 12 intervening years between the original manuscript and this update, the world has seen a lot. What proved to be history's longest bull market peaked amid a truly unprecedented event—the economic lockdowns in response to COVID. Then came four-decade highs in inflation, a swift spate of Fed rate hikes, and two wars. Markets went from history's longest bull market to the shortest, sharpest bear market ever. Then to a brief bull market and a shallow, recession-less bear market that included steep declines in allegedly "safe" Treasury bonds. And, as I type, a bull market. This second edition updates all the data, examples, and logic for these events. Through it all, an amazing thing happens: The lighthouse this book counseled you to build years ago still stands, helping guide you toward your future prosperity.

Of course, then as now, this book isn't a personal financial plan for you. No book can be. I don't know you. I don't know your goals. I don't know your health, comfort with volatility, or any other crucial factor that goes into crafting a retirement investing strategy for you.

But this book can give you the basic tools to craft a plan. It can help inform your conversations with a financial professional, should you choose to use one. It can give you a better framework for how you think about the long journey ahead, whether you are at day one in your career and starting to put money away for the far future or drawing on savings you accumulated, maybe even in what seems like the distant past.

That framework for thinking—giving you the tools to build your own lighthouse—was my aim a decade-plus ago in writing this. They remain so today with this second edition. I hope you enjoy it—and find it helpful in planning your path to prosperity.

Ken Fisher
Dallas, Texas

Acknowledgments

This book, my ninth, is a bit of a departure for me. Normally, I write on the capital markets aspect of investing—what to buy and when; why and how to avoid tactical investing errors. This is my first book focusing almost solely on the decisions that must be made *before* you get to that point—and very critical decisions they are. So much later investing success depends on getting those big, early, long-lasting decisions right.

When I first wrote this book, the scars of 2008's huge and painful bear market had many looking backward instead of forward at the rest of their (potentially, very long) investing time horizon, so the time seemed apt to write a book on the planning side of investing. That was the original inspiration. But in rereading it, I still think many things covered here are vital for new investors, high-net-worth investors, and those of all ages to grasp, understand, and get in their bones.

Books are a hobby for me, not a vocation. And as the years pass, I find more of my leisure time getting appropriated by family (a wonderful thing). So my supporting cast is of utmost importance—these books could not happen without them. First, I must thank and acknowledge Lara Hoffmans, who wrote the original draft of this book over a decade ago. That it has stood the test of time is evidence of the quality of her work.

A hearty thanks is also due to Chris Ciarmiello, who wrote most of the updated text for this latest version. His excellent work made this update so easy for me—a true breeze.

Acknowledgments

A hearty thanks, also, to Todd Bliman and Elisabeth Dellinger for helping manage the project, as well as reviewing and consulting on updates. They saw this across the finish line in the end and made sure this version hit all the right notes.

Data updates for this second edition were the work of Fisher Investments Research Specialist Jimmy Morris and Portfolio Evaluation Analyst Michael Gigantelli. Their prompt, timely assistance with this update is greatly appreciated. Additionally, for valuable consultations on this update, thanks are due to both Fisher Investments Portfolio Management Communications Vice President Nate Halisky and Financial Planning Vice President Kevin Goyert, CFP®.

Fisher Investments' Investment Policy Committee members Aaron Anderson, William Glaser, Michael Hanson, and Jeff Silk join me in making portfolio decisions for my firm's clients. They didn't contribute to the book, but they certainly contribute to how we implement the approach outlined here for the benefit of clients. CEO Damian Ornani runs the day-to-day business of my firm—which couldn't be successful without the combined efforts of those five fine gentlemen.

Many thanks to Jeff Herman, my excellent agent, who led me to John Wiley & Sons, Managing Editor Stacey Rivera, and the rest of the team: Delainey Henson, Kevin Harreld, and Shridhar Viswanathan.

Last and most important, thank you to my wife, Sherrilyn, whose support and patience I'm eternally grateful for.

Ken Fisher
Dallas, Texas

CHAPTER 1

What? Me? Retire?

W ho needs a book on retirement investing?

Maybe you're younger—early in your career. To you, retirement investing is something you do *when* you're retired. Or close to it. Too boring to think about now. Too far away to bother. (Wrong.)

Maybe you're in retirement now or close to it. And you already have a plan. Can't be bothered. But are you sure your plan is sufficient? What's more, are you sure your plan is in fact a plan—and not just a collection of tactics?

Either way, however old you are or however far along in your career, the time to think about a retirement investing plan is *now*. This book isn't just for retirees or soon-to-be retirees but **anyone who plans to retire ever**—whether that's next week or in three decades.

The Imagined Dichotomy

Many investors and even some professionals distinguish between *financial* planning and *retirement* planning—like they're two distinct phases, or the two are, inherently, radically different.

But in my view, this imagined dichotomy is wrong—this idea that you should invest one way for a period of years and then you need a whole separate set of rules upon hitting some milestone.

For most investors, whether you're 22, 52, or 82, financial planning *is* retirement planning *is* financial planning. Whether you're saving your first dollar or your four millionth (good for you!), you should consider the ultimate long-term purpose for your money, which, for many investors, is to provide for them (and their spouse) in retirement and/or leave something behind for the loved ones, a beloved cause, etc.

But maybe not! Maybe this doesn't apply to you. You don't need to think about the ultimate purpose for your money now. Maybe you're heir to a billion-dollar fortune. Your future is amply covered, you don't want to think about it, you bought this book only to level your kitchen table, and your entire purpose in life is to fritter. Fine! But for most everyone else, if you're holding this book, however old you are, you should be thinking, now, about your future prosperity.

Two Goals ... and Some Non-Goals

I have two primary and very specific goals with this book—and some specific goals this book is *not* aimed at.

First, I hope to help you stop thinking about investing in a spliced-up way—that you should invest for a number of years one way, and then one day, a buzzer goes off signaling it's time to think about retirement. No! Instead, from the first time you fund an IRA or otherwise set money aside, I hope to get you thinking not just about retirement but about investing for your whole life. And if you haven't been thinking that way all along, there's no time like the present to change.

Sure, there can be nearer-term goals beyond retirement. You're young and newly married and want to save for a new home. Or you want to save to upgrade to a bigger home. Or you're saving for your kid's college or *your* college or a boat or whatever floats that boat. However, these should all be seen and felt as near-term sidesteps on what's otherwise a lifelong pursuit.

So I want you, right now, to stop thinking about *investing* and *retirement investing* and start thinking about investing for the entirety of your life. I want you to think about making plans now that increase the odds you achieve your goals, whatever they may be. (Heck, at this point, you may not even be able to easily and clearly express what those goals are! Or know what's feasible. This book will help there, too.)

By the same token, if you start thinking, now and always, about the long future ahead (instead of chopped-up phases), that doesn't mean nothing ever changes about how you invest as you near retirement. It might! But not just because on Tuesday, you woke up, went to work, went to a good party in your honor—and on Wednesday, you were *retired*. And now there are new rules because you're *retirement investing*. No—this is selling yourself short and potentially exposing you to investing errors that may unwittingly increase a key risk to you long term.

Maybe, as part of your longer-term thinking, you will need to make a change, whether big or small, at some later point. Maybe multiple changes. But your circumstances and goals should determine when that change (or those changes) is (or are) made, not just a circled date on the calendar.

An investing shift—big or small—might be justified ... but perhaps 7 or 10 years *before* you retire. Or 5 years after. Or 12 years after. Or ... or ... or ... or ... But you won't know that if you think the primary driving factor is your retirement party, not your goals and the effort to increase the likelihood you reach them.

Benchmark for Better Results

My second goal is helping you choose a proper benchmark. If you get nothing else out of this book, I hope you understand what a benchmark is, how important it is, and what goes into choosing a proper one.

Maybe right now you don't even know what a benchmark is. That's fine—we cover that much more in Chapter 3 and beyond. But for now, think of your benchmark as an essential investing lifeline. It's a road map, showing your planned route—and how to take detours when necessary. It lets you know how you're doing—if you're going too slow or even too fast or getting lost in the weeds or utterly turned around. It can help you stay disciplined (an incredibly important yet often overlooked facet of successful investing). Overall, the benchmark, picked properly, can increase the odds you achieve your long-term goals.

The first operative word is *properly*.

Far too many investors invest without a benchmark at all—never mind a proper one. They effectively stick their thumbs in the air, hitchhiking along with whatever tactics suit their fancy at a point in time. What's worse, they may not even realize they're doing that! They may assume they've got a rock-solid plan that makes good and smart sense—but if you don't have a benchmark (and if you don't know what a benchmark *is*, then you don't have one), the odds increase you may be meandering. And meandering is a bad path to prosperity.

It can happen! You can stumble into a portfolio that can provide the kind of life you need down the road through luck (sometimes known as *dumb luck*—and in effect, the same thing). But if given the choice between dumb luck and smart planning, my guess is most folks would opt for the smart planning.

And the benchmark being proper *for you* is key. If your goal is to drive from New York City to San Francisco, a map of Düsseldorf won't help much. A map of the US Eastern Seaboard is better but still falls short. You need a map that consistently shows the way and highlights the "do not go" areas. A good benchmark can do that.

Second operative words: *increase the odds*.

I say that (or some variation) throughout the book—the aim is to increase the odds you reach your goals. Note I didn't (and won't) say, "The aim is to definitely get you to your goal—I promise." Why? This is a book on investing. Investing in anything requires some risk—which type (there are myriad) and how much depend on your unique goals and circumstances.

Plus, no one can guarantee you anything. US Treasurys are guaranteed in the sense they're backed by the full faith and credit of the US government, and so long as the US government doesn't go belly up, you *will* get your principal back, plus interest. (And no, I'm not one of those who thinks the US is teetering on a precipice. You need a different sort of book for that.) But you *can still lose money* investing in Treasurys if you don't hold them to maturity. (Never mind inflation's effect—which we cover later.)

No one can guarantee you reach your goals. Not even you can. First, investing involves the risk of loss. Can't escape it. You could bury cash in your backyard and avoid all *volatility* risk—but you're still fully exposed to *inflation* risk. This means having to earn and save a lot more, and/or downgrading your future cash needs and/or not minding your purchasing power being eroded over time. (More in Chapter 4.)

That's the investing side, but there is also tremendous room for your brain to go haywire. If you have wildly unrealistic goals (e.g., "I want my money to double every year!" or "I want market-like returns but don't want to ever experience downside!"), that can decrease the odds you reach them. If you have a great plan and a sound strategy and a proper benchmark but not the fortitude to stay disciplined over the long haul, that also decreases your odds.

Your aim should be taking steps to identify goals, picking a benchmark and a plan and then doing what's necessary to stick to it. And my aim is to help you. That's how we *increase the odds*.

Again, this should be a deliberate undertaking, whether you go it alone or with a professional. Not only is it critical you pick a proper benchmark, but you must also understand the risk and return characteristics of that specific benchmark. You must understand them so you can be prepared (mentally

7

and emotionally) to accept the shorter-term volatility of your benchmark. (And yes, unless investing in cash, all benchmarks will experience shorter-term volatility.) And no matter how prepared you are, shorter-term downside volatility can sometimes be difficult to experience. But the value of a benchmark is it can aid you in remaining disciplined (as discussed further in Chapter 3). What's more, this is where a good professional can add value as well—in helping you remain disciplined to your strategy when the going gets tough.

The Non-Goals

Full disclosure, right up front: This book won't make a benchmark recommendation or an asset allocation recommendation or provide a specific investing plan. You may think, "Then why the heck buy and read this book if it's not giving me a concrete plan?"

Because no book can do that. No Internet article can do that. They may try! But in my view, what they're giving are cookie-cutter static plans or lists of rules of thumb (which are often partially or wholly wrong).

Fact is, I don't know you. I can't hope to know you via this format.

Instead, my aim is to *help you help yourself* pick a benchmark that's the foundation for a plan that's right for you. Or if you choose to work with a professional, give you a framework for improving the dialogue you have with him/her/them.

This book also isn't meant to supplant professional advice or serve as a shortcut to retirement planning. There *are* no shortcuts. No doubt, many readers hope such a book exists. In my view, it doesn't. Rather, my goal is to share some general principles and concepts I believe can help you (or you and your chosen professional) better shape your long-term investing plan. No book ever written (nor any group of books together) is the silver bullet to investing success. I say that with confidence, having written nine books and read hundreds more, at least. And whether you set up your plan on your own or with a professional, that process should be careful and deliberate.

Also, this book isn't on the nitty-gritty of portfolio management—how to pick securities and which ones and when. To cover that would require vastly more pages. Plus, that's generally what my other books are about. Read this one first, and when you're ready, read *The Only Three Questions That Still Count* (my 2007 book, updated in 2012). But you can't start deciding what to buy and sell and when and why if you don't have your road map—your benchmark.

Definitions and a Pencil

There are other aspects of financial/retirement planning this book won't address. If you're confused about what those aspects are, the official definition of *financial planning* is ... well ... there isn't one.

Financial planning can be a catchall for a wide array of financial services. To call yourself a "financial planner" may not require any testing or specific certification—depending on what you do or sell.

Yes, there *is* certification for financial planners who choose it—like the "certified financial planner" (CFP). And there are professional financial planning organizations. And if you want to be a financial planner *and* sell mutual funds or insurance, you must adhere to certification and testing standards for those specific product categories.

Yet there's no official definition for what a *financial plan* is. A financial plan may include things like a budget or maybe some long-range projections based on a variety of assumptions. Or a financial plan might address insurance and estate planning needs. Or there could be some investment advice included. Or not! Or a planner might also be an accountant (whether certified or not) and do taxes. Or ... or ... or ...

The murkiness doesn't mean financial planning services are *bad*. My firm offers them to clients. Depending on your personal situation, getting advice on insurance analysis, estate planning, tax strategy, Social Security and Medicare usage, and other decisions could be beneficial.

That said, the financial plan is often a way for practitioners to get a foot in the door and sell something (or somethings) else that pays a commission—like a mutual fund, insurance, annuity, or tax services. Because being a commission-based or fee-based salesperson is often more lucrative than being a fee-based planner getting paid to do one plan, once, for a household—simply because such a strategy requires a relatively nonstop influx of new customers, which can be tough to keep up long term. Not that there aren't plenty of fee-based planners making a fine living doing just that. My firm doesn't offer any commission-based products, but it's up to others how they want to run their businesses.

But in general, when folks talk about financial planning, the major buckets included are investing, saving and budgeting, and insurance and estate planning.

There are plenty of excellent books on how to budget and save, and I don't have anything else to say on this you can't get from them. Nothing wrong with budgeting! And nothing wrong with those books. *Everyone* should have a budget. Many people don't budget, and many of them do just fine. (They'd probably do better with a budget, though.) But this book isn't meant to hector you into making your own coffee instead of spending $7 at a fancy coffee shop.

As for insurance, I can say it's normal for young people to be under-insured (not good) and older people to be over-insured (also not good)—though that's not universally true. Remember, too, insurance is just that—protection against some form of loss. You pay for it based on the insurance firm's opinion of the risk associated with that loss and how likely it is. Insurance *is not* investment. The goals for your insurance and investments often are and (at times) *should be* at odds.

For example, if you're a younger person with many earning years ahead of you, it may make sense to buy life insurance—as cheap as you can get it. Particularly if you have children. (Term life insurance can be very cheap and easy to get.) If you die tragically at age 40, aside from emotional devastation for your family, that can have long-term financially devastating effects, too. And not just if you're the primary wage earner! If you or your spouse is a full- or part-time stay-at-home parent, don't underestimate the value of that service—or the cost to replace it.

With insurance, you necessarily want to think, "What happens if I get hit by a bus next week? Next year? In five years? In 10?" With your investments, you may be thinking, "What if I live to be 90? Am I doing the right thing to ensure my money doesn't run out before then?" Those two things are diametrically opposed and have very different implications.

And you most certainly want to have a will—particularly if you have children. You can now find cheap estate planning resources online, or you can find someone who specializes just in estate planning (and/or insurance).

Estate planning might make you think of the dreaded estate tax, although this doesn't trigger until you reach estates of about $13.6 million in 2024. Even beyond this, though, Uncle Sam hovers over many aspects of financial planning. Which type of retirement account or accounts you open 401 (k), Roth IRA, Standard IRA, and beyond carries tax implications affecting the likelihood you reach your financial goals. It is the same for how you time and sequence withdrawals from these accounts. Appendix E includes a high-level view of various withdrawal strategies, but permutations abound depending on personal circumstances. A tax professional can offer more tailor-made advice than this book can.

Budgeting, insurance, tax planning, estate planning— these are all important considerations. But this book focuses almost exclusively on the investing aspect.

Why? I'm an investor—have been my entire adult life. It's my specialty and that of the firm I founded. It's what I wrote about in my monthly *Forbes* columns from 1984 through 2016, making me the longest-tenured columnist in the magazine's history. It's what I continue to write about today in regular columns published in more than two dozen countries across five continents. And it's the subject of 11 books I've written. This is my wheelhouse. Though insurance is important, I'm not sure you want to hear what I have to say about buying it. For that, you want an insurance expert. Ditto for estate planning.

In the same way, if you need heart surgery, you see a cardiac specialist. If you have diabetes, you go to an endocrinologist. If you get cancer, you see an oncologist. Specialization is so common in the medical field now, no one thinks much about it—but that same concept is often less highly regarded elsewhere. Physicians (like many capitalists) seem to have grasped the concept if you specialize in everything, you often do nothing truly well.

And yet, it wasn't always that way. The medical field is as old as humanity, but the idea doctors should specialize is relatively new. My grandfather, Arthur L. Fisher, graduated in 1900 in the fourth graduating class from Johns Hopkins Medical—a real pioneer at an institution that defined medical innovation then and now. He did post-graduate work in Europe and specialized in orthopedics at a time specialties didn't really exist. Johns Hopkins was on the forefront of that, too—its founder and subsequent caretakers understood the power of depth of understanding.

Make no mistake: There's nothing wrong with an internist or a general practitioner. They can help with diagnosing and send you in the right direction—or at least recommend a next step. But you want the specialist to actually operate on you when an operation is called for. (And the internist doesn't want to operate either—not their thing.) And you shop around for the one you think is best for you (as much as you're able—let's not get into a discourse on the state of US health care). You probably don't have the GP down the block operate on your brain tumor, just because they're conveniently located.

Specialization of labor is a hallmark of capitalism and the lifeblood of global trade. It's what has allowed for rapid innovation of life-extending and life-improving goods and services. You can't have a smartphone or smart TV, a car, a home, or an ice cream cone without specialization of labor. You can't have ibuprofen or a vaccine. Heck, you probably can't get your taxes done or take a college course. You can't go online and read email. You wouldn't be reading this book!

If you've not read Leonard E. Read's short essay "I, Pencil," find it online and read it. You've probably not thought much about pencils since you were in grade school. And you may have never thought about why a pencil exemplifies the myriad benefits of free-market capitalism. But if you tried to make a pencil from scratch, the massive societal benefits of specialization of labor and profit motive would become abundantly clear almost instantaneously.

That is why I, as a longtime professional investor, founder, and Executive Chairman of a firm that manages hundreds of billions of dollars for other people and large institutions, am writing on just the investing part of retirement planning. It is my specialty and that of my firm. You want specialists for things this important.

Start Immediately. Now. Right Away

This is (or should be) beyond obvious, but the sooner you start saving and investing, the more money you likely have down the road.

You've probably heard that endlessly, but my sense is many folks don't get, in their bones, the power of compounding interest.

Here's the magic demonstrated. If you're 25 now and plan on retiring at 65 and do *nothing* but max out your IRA contribution each year ($7,000 as of 2024, or $8,000 if you're 50 or older) and just match equities' long-term annualized return of 10%, at age 65 you'd have more than $3.4 million. That's without a 401(k) or any additional savings. And that's assuming the IRS won't increase the IRA contribution level ever again (which it probably will).

We go into this more in Chapter 7, but the more you save early, the more you juice the power of compounding interest. Save just an additional $2,000 a year, and you end up with nearly a million more. Max out your 401(k)—currently $23,000—and you could wind up with far more ... over $11 million ... before even considering employer matching contributions. It's not a paltry amount for a 25-year-old just starting out, but it's not a ridiculous amount. *Particularly* since the entire contribution for that 25-year-old may be pre-tax, lowering their tax liability and did I mention the $11 million? Or you could contribute to a Roth 401(k). That isn't pre-tax, but the withdrawals and growth are tax-free. $11 million tax-free will certainty help fund retirement goals.

That's serious money. Now, it relies on historical long-run returns repeating. That isn't assured, but so long as the profit motive drives businesses to invest and innovate, the chances equities get something like the historic long-term average annual return over the 40 years ahead are pretty good.

If you're young and can't save much now, start smaller, but commit to increasing the amount saved when you get raises. The sooner you start, the sooner you get the compound-interest snowball rolling.

Plan Your Prosperity

Why is this book *Plan Your Prosperity* and not *Plan for Prosperity*? First, creating a retirement investing plan is very personal.

Magazine surveys and static rules of thumb aren't sufficient, in my view. Your benchmark (and, therefore, strategy) should be personal to you and driven by your circumstances and goals.

Second, like beauty, prosperity is in the eye of the beholder. What's prosperity to you may not be to someone else. This isn't about getting over some arbitrary line in the sand or my drawing one for you. This is about determining what you want to achieve, checking to see if it's reasonable, and then doing what you can to increase the odds you get there. That's *your* prosperity.

It might mean saving $500,000 for retirement, $1 million, $7 million, or $73.546 million. Whatever your view of prosperity, you need a plan.

You also need realistic expectations. If you earn $80,000 a year and spend $79,000, you likely won't get to $73.546 million. It's important to understand that now—so you can adjust your budget or get a higher-paying job or prepare your spouse for relatively reduced living standards. Also, pie-in-the-sky expectations can hurt you much worse if you end up deceived by a financial Ponzi con artist. (More on that in Chapter 5.)

To get you to your plan for prosperity, the book walks you through how to think about some key issues. The final chapter consolidates the high points for easy reference later. A word of caution: You could skip to the end and read just the high points, but in my view, it's critical to understand what's driving a good plan and why. Otherwise, it's too easy to go astray.

Make no mistake, creating a sound retirement investment strategy requires some serious homework. To start, it requires a good, hard, honest assessment of where you are and where you want to go. Often, folks don't like being that brutally honest with themselves about money. Thinking about how much money you need 10, 20, or 37 years from now isn't as enticing as thinking about a hot stock you want to buy today—or a hot car! But if you want to get to your prosperity, it's critical.

Then, too, creating the plan won't be nearly as hard for most people as sticking to it. Investing—no matter what you invest in—can be difficult because our unruly brains often lead us astray (in ways and for reasons covered more later in the book). All the more reason to do the work now to create a long-term plan—to counteract your baser instincts, which often are terrible investing guides. So here we go.

CHAPTER 2

My Goals Are ... What?

Before you can make a plan or even think about a benchmark—whether you're going it alone or working with a professional—you must know what your goals are.

The good news for most individual investors is their goals can be stated fairly simply. That doesn't mean achieving them is simple! (It probably won't be.) But your goals should be easy to state and understand.

But have you ever tried articulating them? Does it take you a PowerPoint presentation with fancy graphics and piles of jargon? Or can you articulate them clearly to your spouse or your 90-year-old mother? And are you confident anyone you work with will clearly understand your goals? And nothing will get lost in translation?

This chapter covers:

- Common investing goals and how to articulate them
- How to know which goals are appropriate for you
- One goal that sounds great in theory but is greatly misunderstood
- Why considering inflation's insidious impact is critical to long-term success

Why Is This So Hard?

Why do some investors find simply stating their goals so difficult? My guess is, in part, the financial services industry itself hasn't always been exactly helpful.

The industry is often much maligned. I have my own gripes with it, but for all its faults (every industry has them), it does provide a vital service. Done right, investment professionals help investors increase the odds they reach their long-term goals.

There is, however, a dizzying array of financial products—for every need, real or imagined. And more every year! Financial innovation is a nonstop process. And overall, a good one. Over time, it has provided wider access to global capital markets, increased liquidity, more transparency, better price discovery, speedy online trading, cheaper transactions, etc.—which, overall, benefit more and more people. Good things! But with so many more products coming to market and with so many people selling those products, it's no wonder folks often see themselves as having hugely multifaceted and sometimes conflicting goals.

Not everyone needs a professional. Maybe some investors have smaller pools of money right now, making professional help less cost efficient. And many investors have the knowledge, experience, and fortitude to do it on their own. They know what's appropriate for them, do research, go online, buy some decent securities, and don't jigger much unless jiggering seems appropriate. They have ice water in their veins and don't get swayed by the vagaries of near-term performance, which can vary a fair bit depending on the strategy.

Plus, over long periods, few professional money managers beat their chosen indexes. Some long-term legends have done it. But even if money managers don't meet or beat their benchmarks, good professionals can provide an exceedingly valuable but all-too-often underestimated service—helping their clients stick with the correct strategy.

There are myriad mistakes investors make. Many of the books I write focus at least in part on common investing errors and how to better avoid them. My view is investing well is at least two-thirds about not making mistakes. If you can avoid common errors most investors make, you can lower your error rate on average and get better results over the long term.

Said another way: If you invest long term, you *will* make mistakes. You should expect it. The goal should be identifying errors you're likely to make and trying to avoid those. And failing to stick with a strategy is a major error many investors make. Repeatedly. Maybe you've already made this mistake. Maybe a few times! And maybe you don't even realize it. (Many folks don't.)

Why don't investors stick with a strategy? Your brain and the way it reacts to problems evolved long ago when we didn't have fast Internet connections with stock prices flashing in our faces (or grocery stores, indoor plumbing, etc.). Our brains were hardwired through millennia to deal with problems of survival—not with something as counterintuitive as capital markets.

Folks who study behavioral finance have identified many cognitive errors—instinctual behaviors learned from our stone-age ancestors—that plague investors. And often, multiple ones are at work at any one time. For example, investors often suffer from *myopic loss aversion.* This is hypersensitivity to near-term losses or even just fear of losses in general. It can cause investors to take action to avoid the near-term possibility of pain—*even if taking that action might cause much greater pain down the road.* You might think of this like the "flight" instinct, and it's deeply ingrained—no one wants to get mauled by saber-toothed tigers.

Also at work in investors' brains (often the same investor, and sometimes following rapidly after the myopic loss aversion) is *overconfidence.* That saber-toothed tiger might be scary, but darn it, one kill will feed your family for two months, and its coat is nice and warm. That might seem worth the risk of facing down the beast, armed with just a flimsy, stone-tipped stick. Big risk can mean big reward. That kind of overconfidence helped our ancestors confront seemingly indominable challenges. But it can whack you in investing.

A bit simplistic but perhaps useful way to think of those (and many other) cognitive errors is they tend to fall into the broad buckets of "greed" and "fear." Which one is motivating you now? And why? Just because you feel fearful doesn't mean the flight instinct is right and won't cost you later. And just because you feel greedy doesn't mean that instinct is right, either. Thousands of years ago, running when fearful probably served early humans well. In investing, the reverse is often true. After all, Warren Buffett popularized the (very often true) statement, "You should be greedy when others are fearful and fearful when others are greedy."

And investors aren't prone to just feel fearful forever or greedy forever. A strategy investors view as smart and right for them might seem like snoozeville after a couple or three years of big, back-to-back double-digit returns—as can happen in bull markets. Then, getting big positive returns can seem easy to some. *Too* easy, so they may be tempted to amp up risk to juice portfolio returns by going heavily into a hot category or two.

This often happens right before that hot category cools (like Energy in 1980, Tech in 2000, Financials in 2008, or Tech again in 2021). After the hot category crashes—and with it, maybe the entire market—those same investors who thought their strategy too staid may now decide they're done with stocks forever and want nothing but (presumed) low-risk instruments.

But after every bear market comes a bull market, world without end, Amen. And then those investors who thought they'd never buy another stock may eventually think their so-called low-risk strategy is for the birds, and now they want to ratchet up risk again.

This can happen over and over again as investors in-and-out of various vehicles—chasing heat' and getting burned—flip-flopping between greed and fear. The truth is, if a strategy (done right) is appropriate for your long-term goals (which we'll get to in a bit), that strategy should remain appropriate for you no matter the market condition.

Sure, the tactics can change depending on market conditions, and a good strategy allows for flexibility. But wholesale changing your entire strategy (i.e., your benchmark) every few years is a recipe for disaster.

How can you know? Each year, DALBAR, a Boston-based financial services market research firm, releases a report on a variety of investor behaviors. Its research shows the average equity mutual fund investor tends to hold funds from about two-and-half to five years—typically more when bull markets are running and less when bear markets strike.[1] That may not even be a full market cycle! Heck, the bull market that started in 1990 lasted over nine years. The one starting in 2009 lasted almost 11![2]

But who cares if the results are good, right? Except they aren't good—just the reverse. Through 2023, the average equity fund investor averaged just 5.23% annualized returns over the past 25 years, while the S&P 500 (the benchmark for the funds they measured) over that time annualized 7.56%—a 2.33% annualized lag to the benchmark over 25 years.[3] Over the past 10 years, the gap more than doubles to 4.79%![4]

Now, that isn't to say the mutual funds investors inned-and-outed matched the performance of the S&P 500 on average. They probably didn't! But on average, those funds likely did much better than the investors themselves. Myriad studies have shown funds do better—usually much better—than their individual investors because investors in-and-out. An average three-, four-, or even five-year holding period likely hurts much more than it helps.

It isn't just equity fund investors who do this. Bond fund investors typically hold their funds on between two to four years, according to DALBAR's research.[5] And while the Barclays Aggregate Treasury Index—a common bond benchmark—returned 3.42% annualized over the past 25 years, the average bond investor *barely* notched positive returns, annualizing a mere 0.09%.[6]

No, not every money manager you hire will beat its stated benchmark—whether you buy funds or hire a discretionary manager. And maybe your goal isn't beating a certain index, whether it's equity, fixed income, or a blended index. But just staying disciplined to an appropriate strategy and not inning-and-outing can materially improve your long-term results. And having a third party can help.

Your Investing Goals, Simply

In my view, for most individual investors, your high-level goals can be expressed very simply. When you boil it down, the vast majority of individual investors typically have one of the following four goals:

- Growth
- Cash flow
- A combination of growth and cash flow
- Capital preservation (but this is misunderstood and often inappropriate for many investors)

Straightforward. Simple! Again, that doesn't mean achieving them is simple. But by determining what your goals are, you're one big step down the road of building a proper retirement investing plan. That's perhaps your most important job as an investor: Clearly define reasonable goals, and then determine periodically if the road you're on can get there.

We'll go over these goals more in later chapters to help you better understand what's reasonable to expect, whether your current portfolio size and current savings plan are sufficient, and, perhaps more important, how to make sure your plan (whether you devise it or someone else does) increases the likelihood you achieve your goals. But let's briefly review each goal.

Growth

Growth is growth. Seems easy—growth! You have something now; later, you have more. But how much growth is right for your objectives and needs?

For example, equity-like growth might match your goals. (We talk more about what's reasonable to expect from equities in Chapter 5. It's critical to consider what's reasonable because product peddlers and, worse, con artists often prey on those with unrealistic growth goals. A bad product can easily disappoint and set you back from your goals. But if you're taken in by a scam, your loss can be total. Beware unreasonable growth goals.) Or you might think you want to just keep pace with inflation. You may not think of that as growth, but even just keeping pace with inflation requires some growth.

Cash Flow

A common statement folks make about their investments is "I need this to provide for me in retirement." They want their portfolio to kick off enough cash to cover living expenses— now or in the future, partially or wholly. Maybe those are *your* living expenses (when I say "your," I'm including your spouse, if you have one). Maybe they're yours and/or living expenses of a loved one—a parent, a child still living with you.

Whatever happens to the absolute value of your portfolio— whether it grows, shrinks, or depletes—this goal is about aiming for the portfolio to survive long enough to kick off whatever cash flow is needed.

Also, I say *cash flow* instead of *income* for a reason—there is a difference, which we'll cover more in Chapter 6.

Some Combination Thereof

Then there's the growth-and-income goal—a not unusual goal for investors. Folks want their portfolio to kick off some degree of cash flow, and they want their portfolio to stretch to allow for that. Maybe they want a lot of stretching and prefer their absolute (or inflation-adjusted) portfolio size to grow over time, too. Maybe they're more indifferent to portfolio growth and just want to increase the likelihood their cash flow source doesn't run out before they do.

We'll cover this more in later chapters, but, like the pure growth goal, it's critical to understand what's reasonable to expect. If you're taking 20% of your portfolio each year and expect the portfolio to grow above and beyond that on average, your expectations are likely hugely out of whack. (More in Chapters 5 and 6.)

Capital Preservation

The fourth goal, capital preservation, is one that can be a source of confusion for folks. Misperceptions here are common. Capital preservation means preserving the nominal value of your assets. For investors with long time horizons, this is rarely sensible.

Sure, at points in their lives, many may have shorter-term cash-flow needs for one-time large purchases. For example, if you plan to buy a new home sometime in the period ahead—a few months or even a few years—you don't want your down payment to take a near-term whack thanks to stock- or bond-market volatility. And you certainly don't want to tie up that money in something illiquid.

But as a longer-term goal, true capital preservation can mean watching your purchasing power diminish—for reasons that follow.

Potential Pitfall: Capital Preservation and Growth

Even among professionals, there's often confusion about what capital preservation means. Often you hear or read about products, strategies, or tactics that allegedly offer "capital preservation and growth." However, these are two utterly conflicting goals. You can't do them both at the same time—not as a goal.

And if you believe capital preservation is your goal, ask yourself why? Capital preservation means your portfolio value should never lose value—not even on a daily basis—which requires the absence of volatility risk. Sounds nice? Consider: Volatility goes both ways—up and down. You can't get growth without volatility.

Investors, particularly those new to the game but even some grizzled veterans, mistakenly presume bonds protect against downside volatility. Not so! Look no further than 2022. Benchmark US Treasurys—supposedly the safest of the safe—plunged −17.0%, almost as much as US stocks fell.[7]

Bonds are traditionally less volatile in the shorter term than stocks. But risks exist. First and most obviously, bond investors face default risk—and losses can be total. In bankruptcy proceedings, bondholders can sometimes recoup something—but that process can be long and often fruitless.

Some bonds are deemed riskier than others—like so-called junk bonds. Historically, junk bonds pay higher yields, but the risk the firm goes kaput and fails to return principal or reneges on interest payments is higher. But even firms with pristine ratings can and do go bankrupt. Lehman Brothers enjoyed an "A" credit rating right up until the moment it collapsed. The highest rating is "AAA," but "A" is pretty darn good—any CEO would be thrilled. AIG was rated "A," too—right before the US government nationalized it in 2008. Those high ratings didn't guarantee investors anything.

Remember Enron—poster child for corporate malfeasance? It was AAA-rated until CEO Jeff Skilling suddenly and mysteriously stepped down in August 2001. A few months later, the scandal was out, the company was bankrupt, and shareholder value was obliterated—bondholders, too. Credit raters were hoodwinked, as was most everyone else.

Muni bonds also can be worthless if a municipality defaults. Defaults in major municipalities are rare, but they happen. New York City in 1975, Cleveland in 1978, Orange County in 1994, Alabama's Jefferson County in the early 2010s, and Puerto Rico a few years later. Still, a US muni default rarely means investors have a total loss. It can mean investors receive interest payments at a delayed schedule, but utter wipeouts are rare. From 1929 to 1937—the worst period for US municipality defaults (not shockingly, during the Great Depression)—the muni recovery rate was still 99.5%.[8] Pretty darn good.

Complete loss in munis has been rare historically, but munis and *all bonds* experience day-to-day price volatility. Even Treasurys have daily price volatility—and can and have had negative annual returns. Like 2022! True capital preservation would mean holding cash or very near-cash vehicles.

Growth—even mild growth—requires some volatility risk. Can't get upside volatility without the downside. "Capital preservation and growth" sounds phenomenal. Grow your portfolio, and never lose value! Who doesn't want that? Except it's like fat-free steak—near-universally appealing but not possible.

Let me reverse myself for a moment. Capital preservation is possible as a very long-term *result* of a long-term growth goal. If your goal is growth and you have a diversified portfolio of all stocks, odds are, after 20 or 30 years, your portfolio will have grown. Maybe a lot! Maybe it will have doubled a few times! Then, yes, you've preserved your initial capital *and* experienced growth over that very long period.

But in shorter spurts, because your portfolio included volatile assets, there were periods the portfolio was down—on a daily, weekly, monthly, and even yearly basis. But you were okay with that because your goal was growth, and you (presumably) understood growth required some degree of volatility.

So anyone who tells you your *goal* can be capital preservation *and* growth at the same time is providing you a service by unwittingly warning you off. They are either telling you they don't know much about capital markets, or they are trying to deceive you. Either way, run.

Now, some readers may say, "But wait, I could just hold Treasurys to maturity, and that would be some growth. Not a lot of growth—but growth!" True! If you looked at your portfolio value daily (which I don't recommend for anyone who isn't a professional), monthly, or even yearly, you will see some price fluctuation—**yes, even to the downside**. That means if you must liquidate, you can lose money *even holding Treasurys*. However, if you can and do hold to maturity, then that won't matter—and that could be one capital preservation strategy.

However, that's also a strategy that may lag inflation over time. As I write, 10-year Treasurys yield about 4.3%.[5] Long term, inflation has averaged about 3.5%.[9] A strategy where you lend the US government money for 10 years and it pays you 4.3% annually earns you a puny return. If Treasury yields sink a bit or inflation runs a bit hotter, you might lose money.

The 30-year Treasury now yields just 4.5%—also not much higher than inflation's historical trot. And to prevent any near-term price volatility, you *must* hold to maturity. Thirty years is a long time to lock up assets for the high probability of a 1 to 2% return after adjusting for inflation.

Could bond yields rise from here? Sure! But long-term bond yields tend to reflect long-term inflation expectations—so if bond yields rise, it's likely inflation also rises. And rising bond yields make the prices of bonds you currently hold fall. If something happens and you must liquidate, again, you could end up with a loss—not the idea behind a capital preservation strategy.

Inflation's Insidious Impact

Capital preservation often doesn't end up yielding the results folks want because of that silent killer: inflation. But inflation can also get folks who plan for some growth—just not enough.

What Is Inflation?

First, a few words about inflation, because folks often confuse what inflation is and what it isn't.

Milton Friedman famously said, "Inflation is always and everywhere a monetary phenomenon." What he meant was inflation is about money supply—nothing else. Not gold. Not debt. Not trade deficits. Not oil prices. Not any of the other things headlines scream cause inflation. Money supply. If money supply increases faster than economic activity can mop up the excess, prices rise—and prices rising on average *is* inflation. This is often described as "too much money chasing too few goods."

Folks often don't think about money supply, but they should. Irving Fisher's (no relation) famous equation (which Milton Friedman ascribed to) described the relationship between money supply and prices as follows:

$$MV = PQ$$

M is money supply—how much money is out there. Central banks globally control money supply (in part) by raising and lowering key central banking rates (in America, the *fed-funds target rate*). Effectively, when a central bank raises rates, it reduces money supply. When it lowers rates, it increases money supply. Then, too, when a commercial bank makes a loan to you—for a house, for a car, or even through a credit card—that lent money is like money newly minted out of thin air, and that adds to different calculations of *M*.

V is velocity—how fast money moves through the economy. It's like this: You get a car loan from a bank—which is effectively new money introduced to the economy. You give that lent money to the car salesperson. The car salesperson gives a chunk of that money to the car company but keeps some as a sales commission. He uses that commission to pay his mortgage, buy groceries, buy clothes for his kids, and pay insurance premiums. The car company uses the money it received to pay employees but also pays the different firms that produce the microchips, tires, steel, fabric for the car seats, etc. Everyone who receives a bit of money turns around and does another transaction. Or maybe they save it, and the bank uses it to make new loans to other folks! But how fast that money changes hands and then changes hands again is the *velocity*. Sometimes it's faster. Sometimes, like during a recession, economic activity slows, and so does velocity.

P is prices, and *Q* is quantity of goods and services sold—both straightforward.

Don't try to input real numbers. You couldn't if you tried. The equation is meant to be illustrative, but it does show well how money supply and velocity impact prices.

View the US government's COVID response through this lens, and you see why inflation soared in 2021 and 2022. When shutdowns hit, the Fed slashed interest rates and bought up massive amounts of US Treasury bonds and mortgage-backed securities, adding trillions to its balance sheet. The government sent out stimulus checks to households and offered loan programs for businesses. Money, money, everywhere!

But at the same time, lockdowns limited options to spend it. Supply chain disruptions further limited production of goods. Lots of money, too few goods, disrupted output unable to soak up the excess cash ... so *P* spiked.

Big inflation is no fun. Even after price *increases* returned to normal rates in 2024, prices themselves remain far above pre-pandemic levels. So why not simply slash money supply and spur *deflation*—falling prices on average—to erase the big jumps?

Well, falling prices might sound grand at first. They aren't. If you had to choose between mild deflation and mild inflation, you want the mild inflation every day of the week and twice on Sunday—no question.

If prices are in a steadily falling trend, that tends to exacerbate what is likely an already slowing economy. If you know prices will be lower next month, you probably won't make any large ticket-item purchases. You wait for the lower prices later. Firms are the same way. Non-essential economic activity gets put off, so economic activity slows still more.

But prices don't just fall on the things you want to buy, they fall for labor, too—i.e., incomes tend to fall in a deflationary environment. Prices are falling, firms are producing less, you're earning less, and the economy is slowing—probably contracting. Firms probably start cutting costs, which means cutting head count. That's deflation, and it isn't good.

Periods of true, sustained deflation are fortunately rare, at least in major economies like the US. We had some deflation during the 2007–2009 recession, which contributed to and exacerbated the recession. The 2020 flash recession brought big *disinflation*—a slowing of price *increases*—but not broad deflation. It's a bit chicken-and-egg when you talk about deflation and recessions, but it's safe to say without deflation, recessions are usually milder.

Central banks often fight deflation by pumping up money supply. If V falls, you can keep P from falling (or falling as much) by raising M. The aim is to "balance" the equation. And ideally, the rising M gets the V going again, too.

In 2020, shutdowns meant nothing could get V going. No using that extra cash to travel. Or go out to eat. Or go to concerts or ballgames. And people can buy only so many plants and furniture and gizmos and gadgets online.

But when lockdowns lifted, V jumped. Sky-high M, rising V ... that meant P had to soar to balance the equation—especially with supply chain snarls still weighing on Q. Boom! Big "I"—inflation.

On the flip side, when V starts cooking and P starts rising, too, the proper response to prevent overheating inflation is often to rein in M—usually by the central bank's raising rates or some other central bank action (or combination of actions) that can mop up excess money supply.

Lots of people think that's what happened after the Fed jacked up interest rates from March 2022 through 2023 and inflation subsequently waned. I'm not so sure. Why? Banks were sitting on piles of deposits after the lockdowns limited spending options. They kept lending at a healthy rate in 2023 and 2024.[10] So V *kept* moving even as money supply inched lower from late 2022 through early 2024.[11] In my view, inflation ebbing had more to do with supply chain woes unwinding, boosting Q—more goods—and forcing P downward. Rate hikes were a red herring.

Another important point about inflation: Inflation isn't when prices of things you buy rise. Inflation is an *averaging*. In a world of 0% inflation, all prices wouldn't be static. About half would be rising (some faster, some slower) and half falling (some faster, some slower). You may or may not experience the average of all prices, so if the prices of the things you buy most are rising, you may feel that as higher inflation—though overall inflation may be tame.

Figure 2.1 demonstrates this—showing changes in common expense categories over the last 20 years relative to the Consumer Price Index (CPI)—a common measure of inflation. No surprise, college tuition has skyrocketed. Myriad health care categories, too. (Folks like to assign blame for that, and politicians try to solve it, but to my view, their trying to solve things just makes things worse.)

Energy has also risen more than average inflation. Food and beverages and housing have outpaced inflation on average during this period, but barely. Eggs lagged for a long time, but not anymore! (Why eggs are measured here is beyond me. These are government data, and government wonks can be wonkish.) Cars have really lagged inflation, as has apparel.

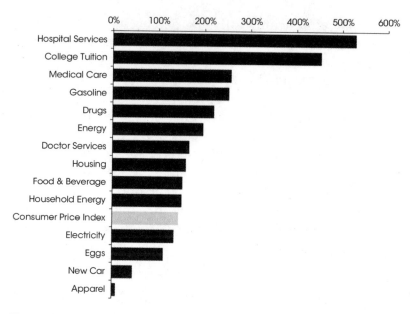

Figure 2.1 Inflation's impact
Source: FactSet, price changes in CPI components, 12/31/1988–12/31/2023.

Mind you, CPI isn't perfect either. It's a measure of a basket of goods—more than 200 item categories (which roughly fall into the major categories shown in Figure 2.1) with hundreds more specific items within each. The aim is to capture the average consumption experience of average Americans. (Good luck with that.) It doesn't include income taxes or property taxes—they're not associated with the purchase of consumer goods. Nor does it include investments like stocks or bonds—they aren't day-to-day expenses.

And the items included change from time to time—eight-track tapes get swapped out for CDs. Then streaming music service subscriptions get added. Then whatever comes next. And you always get folks griping that CPI is out of whack or too jimmied with or governmentally produced, so it is unreliable. Well, yes, all government data should be taken with a grain of salt. But CPI isn't much better or worse than any other way of measuring inflation, and it has a long, consist-ent history. So for measurement purposes, it's fine, though it may not feel like the kind of inflation you're experiencing personally.

This goes back to my point that investors planning for retirement—whether aged 23 or 63—must remember that as they get older, they may consume from those categories that tend to inflate faster. And it's later in life that you likely want the comforts money can buy.

Three-and-a-Half Percent, Compounded

As mentioned, inflation's long-term annual average is about 3.5%.[12] Sometimes inflation has been much higher (the 1970s, early 1980s, and 2021–2023), and sometimes much lower. It is hard to know where it will go in the future, but a safe place to start for a projection is the long-term historical average, know-ing you will go through spurts of higher and maybe lower rates in the future.

Three-and-a-half percent may not seem like much, espe-cially in the wake of recently hot inflation. But don't forget the power of compounding! Long term, this can take a serious whack at your purchasing power.

Say you retired at 65 in 2024 and need about $50,000 a year to cover living expenses. If, over the long future ahead, inflation continues at that average rate, in 2044 when you are 85, you will need almost $100,000 to maintain your quality of life. In 2054, you will need more than $141,000. Figure 2.2 shows the insidious impact inflation has on purchasing power and how much more you need to just maintain the status quo.

Said another way, if you stashed $1 million under your mattress, in 30 years, that money would be worth around $343,000. You did nothing—you experienced no market-like volatility. Yet you still lost huge purchasing power!

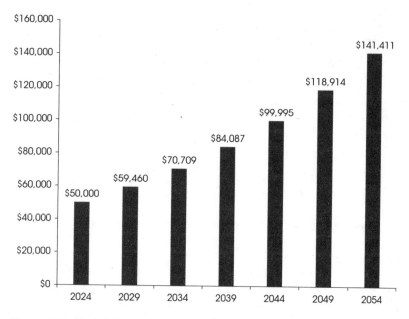

Figure 2.2 Maintaining purchasing power

Source: Finaeon, Inc., as of 2/23/2024. Based on annualized average of US Consumer Price Index, 1/31/1947–1/31/2024.

Now, maybe your cost of living falls—you aren't taking annual ski trips at age 85. But is it possible, as you age, you have other expenses? Pricier ones from those faster-inflating categories like medical care, pharmaceuticals, etc.? This is a major reason many investors do need some growth and true capital preservation often isn't an appropriate goal for folks with long-term time horizons (i.e., most folks reading this book).

Now you have an idea of a clear way to articulate your goals, even if we haven't gotten specific yet. The next chapter covers why having clear goals is so important—because they aid in making the most critical decision of all.

Recap

The first critical step in formulating a retirement investing plan is understanding, and then articulating, your investing goals. At a high level, your goals should be simple (though achieving them likely won't be). Ask yourself what you want to achieve. The answer for nearly all individual investors is likely to be one of the following:

- Growth
- Cash flow (which is different from *income*)
- Some combination of growth and cash flow
- Capital preservation, which is likely a rare goal for readers of this book.

Capital preservation and growth as a singular goal may sound terrific, but these are two conflicting goals inherently at odds. They both cannot be pursued at the same time—anyone telling you otherwise should be avoided.

And never underestimate the insidious impact of inflation, which can seriously erode purchasing power over time.

CHAPTER

3

The Secret Code—Asset
Allocation or Benchmark?

W hy is being as specific as possible about goals so critical for investors? Because goals play a crucial part in determining a *benchmark*.

Many argue (correctly, in my view) the *asset allocation* decision is the most important driver of investment returns. (For relative newbies, asset allocation is the selection of stocks, bonds, cash, and/or other securities, and in what percentages.) And it is! Very important!

But my view is the benchmark effectively *is* your long-term asset allocation decision. It will drive and guide tactical asset allocation decisions and any other later investing decisions you make. Picking a proper benchmark can mean the difference between increasing the odds of having the retirement you plan for and being unpleasantly surprised far too late to do much about it. That's no way to plan your prosperity.

This chapter covers:

- What exactly *is* a benchmark
- Why asset allocation is so important
- The dangers of letting age, and age alone, determine asset allocation
- The difference between a benchmark and a flexible strategy

Benchmark: A Road Map and Measuring Stick

What exactly is a benchmark? A benchmark is your portfolio road map, but it's also a measuring stick for telling you what's reasonable to expect and how good a job you're doing getting there.

But more simply, a benchmark is any well-constructed index. By "well-constructed," I mean market-capitalization weighted (like the S&P 500 index or the MSCI World or ACWI indexes) and not price-weighted (like the Dow).

The Dow is a popular but near-useless stock index that survives mostly out of tradition. I've written extensively on why you should ignore the Dow in my other books, and if you care to read more, I direct you to *The Only Three Questions That Still Count* or Appendix A (which reprints and updates the pertinent chapter from my 2010 book, *Debunkery*). But briefly, the price-weighted construction means a stock with a higher price per share has more influence on index performance than a stock with a lower price per share—even if the lower price-per-share stock is from a vastly larger firm in size (i.e., market capitalization). And year to year, index performance can get heavily skewed—even be arbitrary—based on which stocks split versus which don't and/or whether high- or low-priced stocks do better. Priced-weighted indexes don't reflect economic reality. And you want a benchmark that reflects reality.

Instead, use a market-cap–weighted index—there are plenty. (Most major indexes now are market-cap weighted. The industry has largely moved away from price-weighting, recognizing the major drawbacks.) What's more, the benchmark can be all stock, all fixed income, or blended—60% stocks/40% fixed income or any other mix. It can be all US or all global or all Switzerland or all Sri Lanka. (Though the all-Denmark or all-Sri Lanka benchmarks will be much narrower and therefore likely much more volatile on average—Sri Lanka more than Denmark.)

The S&P 500 Total Return Index is a fine all-US equity benchmark. I believe broader is better—allows for more diversification, which finance theory tells us mitigates risk. And broader allows for more opportunities to enhance performance, if you care to. You can't get broader than a global index, so a good benchmark might be the MSCI World Index, which includes developed economies. Or the MSCI All-Country World Index (ACWI), which adds in developing countries and is even broader.

Once you select a benchmark, it's yours unless something material changes about your situation or goals. That is why it's critical you select carefully (and hence the purpose of this book).

Road Map for a Long Journey

How is the benchmark a road map? It tells you from a high level what to include in your portfolio. If you have an all-equity global benchmark, then your asset allocation should be 100% global stocks—most of the time. If the benchmark is 50% US/50% non-US, your portfolio should be close to that—usually. (We get to exceptions later.) Just as you wouldn't get into your car to drive cross-country without a map or a GPS, you don't want to start managing a portfolio (or let someone else do it) without a benchmark—you can end up lost either way.

Measuring Stick

The benchmark also is a measuring stick. First, if your index has a long enough history (a good one should), it can give you a reasonable framework for shaping forward-looking return expectations.

This means if your benchmark has a long history of annualizing about 6% (as a blended benchmark might), you probably shouldn't count on its annualizing 10% over the 30 years ahead. Now, that doesn't mean a benchmark that *has* annualized 10% over very long past periods (like many broad stock indexes have) *will* annualize 10% over the long period ahead. Far from it! But again, it's about setting reasonable expectations. (More on this in Chapter 5.)

Second, the benchmark lets you measure how you're doing. If your benchmark is the MSCI World Index because your goals indicate you need something close to equity-like returns and for the last five years you've annualized an 8% lag, something about your portfolio execution is probably off.

By the same token, if you beat your index by a wide margin, that may feel great! But it's a major sign you're taking on vastly more than benchmark-like risk. If your benchmark is up 20% in one year (as often happens in a bull market), but you're up 40%—enjoy it! But reassess your strategy—fast. You might have made some big bets—maybe by concentrating heavily in just a few narrow categories or even a few stocks—and been right but also very, very lucky. If you beat your benchmark by a wide margin, remember luck goes the other way, too, and you can just as easily lag it by the same amount, which you won't like.

The benchmark can be your leash, keeping you disciplined. Be very similar to your benchmark and you'll likely get similar-to-benchmark returns. This means you'll endure whatever volatility your benchmark doles out (and yes, bond indexes experience price volatility, too, as 2022 showed in droves). You should expect it. But as long as you stay disciplined to your benchmark, over time, it should get you where you need to go (provided you pick the right one). The more you deviate from your benchmark, the more your returns will differ. And that can be fine! That's how you can outperform it over time, if that's your goal (and if it's done right). But you don't want to aim to beat your benchmark by any more than you're prepared to lag it in a given year.

Picking a Benchmark

If the benchmark is so important, how do you pick it? Your benchmark is determined by your return expectations and cash flow needs (i.e., the goals we discussed in Chapter 2 and will discuss more in Chapters 5 and 6) but also your time horizon—which is how long you need your assets to work for you (discussed more in Chapter 4).

You must also ultimately be comfortable with your benchmark. For example, if the thought of investing in foreign stocks gives you incurable hives, then fortunately for Americans, we have a very deep and broad stock market—a US-only equity benchmark would be fine. (On the flip side, plenty of US investors fret about America's direction and the state of America's economy. If this is you, that's yet another reason to diversify and invest globally!)

If my view is global is better, why is a US-only equity benchmark okay? Because finance theory is clear: All major equity categories, if well-constructed and accounted for properly, should yield similar returns over very long time periods.

However, over shorter periods, index performance can vary wildly. Really wildly! A narrow category like a single country or single sector can be much more volatile year to year than broader markets. For example, many investors remember well the 2000 Tech bubble crash. The Tech-heavy Nasdaq fell 77.9% top to bottom—much more than the S&P 500 (down 47.4% top to bottom) and the MSCI World (down 49.4%).[1] But given longer periods, performance discrepancies generally start fading away—and differences in annualized returns can be attributed to weird, unpredictable statistical quirks, not any inherent category superiority or lack thereof. Fundamentally, no one category is superior to another long term, which means no one category should be expected to have superior return characteristics.

However, finance theory is also clear: The broader the category, the lower the expected volatility. That is why, all else being equal, you should prefer global for the equity portion of a benchmark. You can't get broader than global.

This doesn't mean you won't experience market-like volatility in a global portfolio. You will! There's no avoiding that if you own stocks. But the much wilder swings inherent in narrow categories do get mitigated. (Again, think Tech in 2000.)

Still, if long-term performance should be similar, who cares if your path is especially bumpy? Right? Maybe, except market-like volatility can be trying enough. If you want to increase the odds you stick with an appropriate strategy, amping up volatility probably isn't a good idea. If broad markets are down 30% in any given year (as can happen during a bear market) and you're down 70% or more because you're more concentrated, it can be hard to say to yourself, "Self, I know I'm down much more than the broad market, but I can rest assured that all well-constructed categories should, over long periods, net similar returns." I have been in the business over 50 years, and I know some cool-as-cucumber characters. But I don't know anyone *that* cool.

That's one side of a broad benchmark. The other side is it gives you more opportunities to enhance performance, if you so choose, via active management (which we'll get to in a bit). So, sure, you can use a US-only benchmark—the S&P 500 or MSCI USA is sufficiently broad, and US capital markets are very diversified. But if you can handle foreign investing, the benefits of an even broader benchmark can more than outweigh any initial jitters you might have if you've never gone global before.

The Big Decision: Asset Allocation

So the benchmark is, effectively, your long-term asset allocation decision, which is indeed the biggest driver of portfolio returns, long term. How *big* of an impact is debatable. An academic study by Gary Brinson, Randolph Hood, and Gilbert Beebower posits 90% of your portfolio return is driven by asset allocation—the mix of stocks, bonds, cash, or other securities.

At my firm, we get a bit more granular. We believe about 70% of portfolio return is determined by the high-level stocks/bonds/cash/other securities decision and about 20% is driven by sub-asset allocation decisions—i.e., the *kinds* of securities you are holding. (See Figure 3.1.) Are you holding more big-cap stocks or small? Growth or value? What is your weighting in the major sectors—Energy, Industrials, Materials,

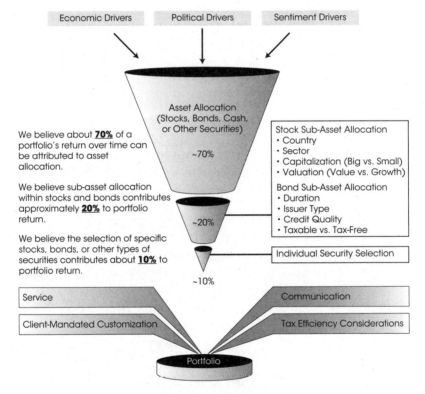

Figure 3.1 The asset allocation impact—70/20/10

Note: Forward-looking return attribution is an approximation intended for illustrative purposes and should not be considered a forecast of future returns or return attribution.

Financials, etc.? What about subindustry selection? For bonds, are you holding Treasurys, municipal bonds, or corporates? What credit rating? What duration? And so on.

But most modern practitioners agree only a relatively small amount of performance over time is driven by the individual security decision—i.e., whether you hold Merck or Pfizer, Coke or Pepsi, a Bank of America or Citigroup bond, etc.

Stock Selection Doesn't Matter?

Does that mean stock selection doesn't matter? No, stock selection does matter, but it's a less critical factor over time than many believe. In short spurts, stock selection can certainly detract from or add to performance. But in a year stocks are down big—like 2001, 2008, or 2022—you might be the world's best stock picker, but knowing that Stock ABC would edge out Stock DEF didn't help much if they were both down big.

What's more, over long periods, stocks tend to act relatively similar to their peer group. Figure 3.2 shows the performance of two Tech titans—Apple and Microsoft. Headlines often play them against one another, as if when one wins the other loses. And they *are* competitors! But as I write,

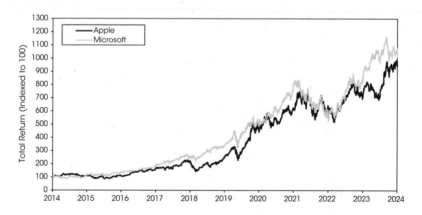

Figure 3.2 Same sector, similar performance
Source: FactSet, as of 11/20/2024. AAPL and MSFT total return, 10/31/2014–10/31/2024.

these two have tracked very closely to one another over the past decade—deviating now and then. Over those 10 years, Microsoft returned 912% and Apple 842%.[2] That's 26.0% annualized to 25.1% annualized. Both are great returns! Agonizing over which one to hold didn't add much to performance.

Stock peers don't always track so closely—there can be huge divergences tied to firm-specific issues, good or bad. But if you lack the time, skill, and/or inclination to do in-depth stock research, know that the bigger decisions on asset allocation and sub-asset allocation will likely pack more wallop over time. In my view, it's easier to pick a selection of stocks that are good representations of the categories you're trying to capture (what's known as "top-down" investing) than sifting through the entire universe of stocks trying to find potential gems (known as "bottom up").

Starting Small. A well-diversified portfolio might mean anywhere between 50 and 70 holdings if you're global—give or take, depending on market conditions. Not long ago, transaction fees would've made that costly for smaller portfolios. That changed when many big brokerages scrapped online trading fees in 2019. Now you can cheaply build out a portfolio of individual stocks.

Or you can use diversified exchange-traded funds, which you can buy and sell just like individual stocks. Their expense ratios—essentially management fees—are often tiny. In a taxable account, Exchange Traded-Fund and individual stock gains and losses are yours. You can carry forward losses forever to offset gains and mitigate your tax bill.

Mutual funds? Active fund costs are typically higher—often much higher. And you could very well have an unrealized loss in a calendar year but still get a bill from the fund manager for capital gains taxes. Why? You have no control over when other fund holders buy and sell—and that can mean increased taxes for you. This is also a factor in ETFs, albeit less common.

The Impact of One on the Whole

Another way to consider the importance of stock selection? If you are well diversified and holding 50 or 70 stocks, if a single stock crashes overnight for some issue unique to that stock—major scandal, hugely surprising earnings miss, whatever—the relative impact on your portfolio is limited. If a position that's 2% of your portfolio goes to zero (pretty rare), that isn't disaster.

Many folks tend to like the concept that single-stock performance gets muted on the downside but then see diversification as a hindrance to getting grand slams on the upside. But they're two sides of the same coin. If you want the opportunity for a stock to go on a wild tear, you must accept that same stock can crater.

With a well-diversified portfolio, you won't experience the giddy highs of putting it all in a stock that pops 1,000% fast (also pretty rare). But you won't utterly be crushed, either. Stocks are volatile enough without dealing with that kind of potential hyper-volatility. Stocks can and do flat line. That's why the bigger, high-level asset allocation decisions are much more impactful over time.

Potential Pitfall: Age Doesn't Equal Asset Allocation

Since asset allocation is so important, advice on the "right" asset allocation abounds. Something you commonly read (or hear): Simply take 100 (sometimes it's 120), subtract your age and that's how much you should have in stocks. Adherents of this rule of thumb believe, if you're 60, you should have 40% stocks, 60% fixed income. If you're 80, it's 20/80. If you're 20, it's 80/20.

Sounds easy! It's a concrete prescription, which a lot of people like. Eliminates any guesswork. Except this rule of thumb presumes the only thing that matters is your age. Not your goals. Not your cash flow needs. Not your time horizon. Not your intended purpose for your money. *Not your spouse!* One input and only one input matters—your birth year.

You can't get much more cookie cutter than that.

See it another way. There are two investors, Jim and Bob, both age 60, each with $2 million saved. The subtract-your-age crew would say, definitively, both should have 40% stocks and 60% fixed income. Identical portfolios!

But hang on! Jim is in excellent health. His wife, Mary, is 10 years younger and also in excellent health—they both love skiing with the kids and play tennis twice a week. They own their own consulting firm, and just now, the business is really taking off. Neither Jim nor his wife plans on retiring for another 10 years. Love what they do! Jim's and Mary's parents are all still alive—Jim's in their 90s and Mary's in their 80s. Mary's dad still golfs six days a week. In 10 years, Mary and Jim plan on selling the business and traveling. They hope the business sale proceeds (which could be sizable) plus portfolio growth and any additional savings will fund their lifestyle. Then, too, it's very important to them that they leave sizable legacies for their grandkids.

Bob is a widower. His parents died in their early 70s of natural causes. He's not very active, likes just spending time with his grandchildren, and recently moved to be closer to them. He's already had two heart attacks and a quadruple bypass. The doctor told him stress was no good for him, so he retired last year. He lives off his portfolio and plans on taking about $100,000 a year in cash flow—the home close to his kids is pricey but worth it, in his view. And he's helping out with private school tuition for the grandkids. He also might need more cash flow in the future for medical costs. His kids do fine, so if there's any money left over for them, that's gravy. He's focused on not being a burden on them and helping out where he can.

Bob and Jim should have identical portfolios?

Jim is planning on at least a 40-year time horizon—the odds Mary lives to her 90s are good. And they don't need cash flow for at least 10 years—and cash flow they take likely funds mostly discretionary spending. And they're *very* focused on growth. Bob isn't—he's focused much more on cash flow now to fund life's necessities. And while he could certainly live another 20 years, he is realistic about his health condition and knows his time horizon is likely shorter.

Is it possible investors with very different goals and time horizons have the same benchmark? Of course! But the driving factor isn't and shouldn't be age alone. It's a factor—it figures into time horizon. But it's just one factor.

Benchmark vs. Asset Allocation: What's the Difference?

You may read this chapter and think, "What's the big difference between benchmark and asset allocation? Aren't they the same thing?"

It depends on which kind of asset allocation you mean! Effectively, your benchmark is your *long-term* asset allocation. You can think of them interchangeably if you like. But whereas your benchmark (and long-term asset allocation) shouldn't change much (if at all), your *tactical* asset allocation can be more flexible.

Why doesn't benchmark change much? The primary determinants of your benchmark are, of course, your return expectations, cash flow needs, time horizon, and any other additional personal preference. These things likely won't change very much or very often.

They *can* change, of course. You might discover later on you need more (or less) income than you previously thought. A 70-year-old widower might remarry a 50-year-old—that would likely change the time horizon. Every year, you should review your goals and time horizon to make sure your benchmark remains the right one for you. But it should take a fairly material change in your circumstances to alter your benchmark.

Why is sticking with your benchmark so critical? Changing it too often could be simple heat chasing—and heat chasing isn't a great way to run a disciplined investment strategy.

Suppose your benchmark is the global MSCI World Index. Maybe you go through a few years where US stocks hugely outperform foreign, so your global index underperforms the S&P 500. Your stone-age brain may tell you that you picked wrong and you're missing out. (Kill saber-toothed tiger! Feed family for months!) After all, don't the past few years of US outperformance tell you US stocks are inherently better than foreign? (Answer: No.) Then, you switch your benchmark— just in time for leadership to rotate to non-US stocks. Leadership of major categories rotates—always and irregularly. Now your S&P 500 benchmark goes through a long period of underperforming most major foreign and global indexes. And then you might be tempted to switch again, just for that relatively hotter index to go cool again. Flip, flop, flip— meanwhile, you're overall underperforming how you would have done had you sat tight with a benchmark that was right for you.

This isn't just hypothetical—for much of the 1980s, non-US stocks hugely beat US stocks, only for US stocks to dominate in the 1990s. Then, during the 2000s, foreign overall led again. The 2010s? You guessed it—US domination. Within, there were shorter spurts when performance flip-flopped irregularly, but neither category has been nor will be permanently superior—nor are outperformance patterns predictive of future patterns.

Know this: Whatever your benchmark, *there will be one (or many) that beats it* over the course of a year or even a few years or even a decade! But recall—if given enough time, all well-constructed equity categories should net similar returns, though traveling different paths.

That is why, once you pick a benchmark, you want to stick with it unless something material happens to your circumstances or goals that would make a change appropriate.

Being Flexible

So your benchmark shouldn't change much, but your tactical asset allocation may. For investors who actively manage their portfolios (or have someone else do it for them), in my view, a flexible asset allocation is beneficial.

Static Isn't a Solution. Many people fall into a trap of having a *static* asset allocation. They may get (hear or read) advice that you should always have fixed allocations of whatever categories—big- and small-cap growth, big- and small-cap value. Or maybe they focus on sectors. Or always 60% stocks and 30% fixed income and 10% cash. Or maybe they focus on categorizing some other way. And they always try to match that static asset allocation, rebalancing occasionally if one category gets out of whack.

This is problematic in a few ways.

First, your benchmark's components aren't static! They are fluid—changing with market conditions. Sometimes growth is in favor, and those categories increase in relative proportion of the benchmark. Sometimes one or a few sectors outperform for a long time, while others underperform—and their relative weights shift.

If you insist on maintaining static allocations, you could end up holding a huge allocation of a sector that underperforms, which would unnecessarily ding your returns. Or you may be unwittingly underweighting a top-performing sector and miss returns that way.

Figures 3.3–3.5 show sector allocation weights of the MSCI World Index as of January 1, 2010, 2015, and 2020. Some sectors didn't shift much; others changed a fair bit.

In 2010, Information Technology—"Tech"—was about 12% of the global stock market. By 2015 it was 13.4%, and by 2020 it had jumped to 17.4%. (As I write in late 2024, that has leapt to almost 25%![5])

The Secret Code—Asset Allocation or Benchmark?

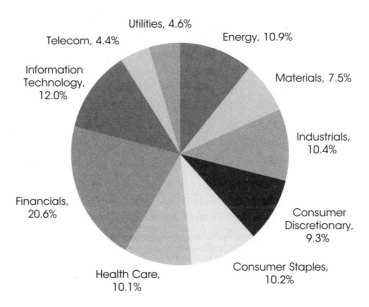

Figure 3.3 MSCI world sector weights: 2010

Source: Adapted from FactSet, as of 11/5/2024. MSCI World Index sector weights as existed on 12/31/2009.

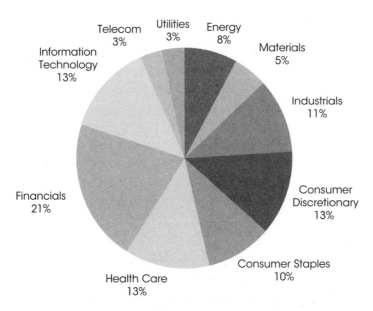

Figure 3.4 MSCI world sector weights: 2015

Source: Adapted from FactSet, as of 11/5/2024. MSCI World Index sector weights, as existed on 12/31/2014.[3]

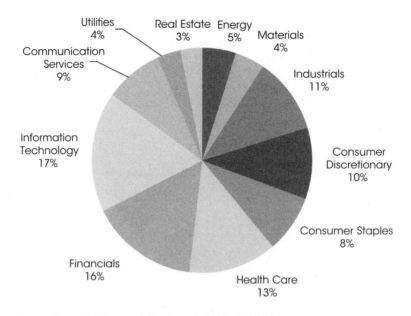

Figure 3.5 MSCI world sector weights: 2020

Source: Adapted from FactSet, as of 11/5/2024. MSCI World Index sector weights as existed on 12/31/2019.[4]

Energy, meanwhile, was 10.9% of the market in 2010. But the next decade wasn't kind to the sector's stocks. New "fracking" technology sent production soaring—creating a supply glut that squashed oil prices. Great for consumers, not so great for Energy stocks, which usually parallel oil prices. By 2015, Energy was down to 8.0% of global market capitalization. By 2020, that sank to 4.9%—less than half what it was a decade prior. (It's even lower as I write.)

It might seem obvious that sectors shift during and after bear markets. But those January 2010–January 2020 moves occurred during history's longest bull market! Economic and sentiment shifts caused sectors to expand and contract, as always. But bookkeeping played a role, too. Two of the world's biggest index providers—MSCI and S&P Dow Jones— reclassified some industries from one sector to another in 2018, citing the changing business landscape.[6] Several big

Tech firms—including Meta (then Facebook) and Google parent Alphabet—were clumped in with the old Telecommunication Services sector, creating a new sector: Communication Services.

So overnight, the tiny Telecom sector—just 3.3% of global market cap in 2015—got a new name . . . and much more clout. By 2020, Communication Services more than doubled to 8.4% of world stocks.[7] Depending on which Telecom and Tech stocks you held before the switcheroo, your portfolio could have skewed sharply from your benchmark. Risky!

So your benchmark changes—and if you're static, you can inadvertently expose yourself to additional benchmark risk. What's more, if you pick static allocations, what's behind those decisions? Are you holding big allocations of categories that *have* performed well in recent years and, thereby, unintentionally chasing heat?

Being flexible lets you more closely reflect your benchmark. The more closely you resemble your benchmark, the lower the odds your performance will deviate and you'll lag. Yes, if your benchmark is down, you'll likely be down, too. But if you have a long time horizon and pick an appropriate benchmark based on your goals, again, the benchmark should, over time, get you where you want to go.

The flipside of that is being static also takes away opportunities to enhance performance. If you, like many investors, want to "beat the market" (henceforth, think of it as *outperforming your benchmark*), that gets tougher to do if you're static.

For example, if you have a strong belief large-cap stocks will outperform small cap or that Energy is likely to outperform the broad market or . . . or . . . or . . . you can shift to overweight those categories. If you're right, you've participated more in a category that outperformed. By the same token, if you think certain categories are likely to underperform, you can underweight those—which also enhances performance relative to the benchmark if you're right.

You won't be right with every decision you make. Far from it! Get used to that right now. You can and will make shifts that are wrong. But the aim isn't to be error free—which no one in the history of professional money management has ever been. (Even the all-time greats made and make tons of decisions that later are proven wrong.) The aim is to be right more than wrong, on average, over your long time horizon—and that can add relative value.

Then, too, there may come a time when you're strongly yet reasonably convinced stocks will be in a sustained bear market. You can also enhance returns relative to your benchmark by shifting heavily out of stocks into fixed income, cash, and/or other securities. Again, this is difficult to do—perhaps the most difficult move investors can make because it may be a significant shift away from the benchmark. You should do so only if you see a big, looming negative that (a) could knock trillions off the global economy and (b) others don't see, meaning stocks haven't yet pre-priced it. Hard to do! You also must have a strict plan to re-allocate aligned with your benchmark well before all negativity abates. The initial upsurge of a new bull market is usually strong—and you don't want to miss that. If you're wrong and defensive while stocks take off, that can crush relative returns. But done well even once or twice during your long time horizon, you can add significant relative value.

If you adhere to a rigid asset allocation, you miss opportunities to enhance performance and manage risk by being flexible. (For how to make those decisions, I direct you to *The Only Three Questions That Still Count*, which gets more into the nitty-gritty of tactical portfolio decision-making.)

Passive or Active?

Now, I will reverse myself a bit. Some investors prefer passive investing to active. Passive investors pick a benchmark and mimic it as closely as possible, often using ETFs or index funds. You *could* call that a form of rigid asset allocation, i.e., never deviating from the benchmark.

Passive investors (when doing it correctly) believe (as I do) that long term, their benchmark will get them where they need to go. They don't have a goal of beating the market; rather, they want to just match it minus any transaction fees, which should be minimal if done right.

Considering investors on average not only don't beat the market but actually badly lag it, just meeting your benchmark is a fine result. A great one! Better than what most investors do and better even than most professionals.

But even if you decide to do passive, if you're mimicking your benchmark using several (or many) securities, you still must check in to make sure your portfolio hasn't gotten out of whack relative to your benchmark—simple rebalancing. Or you could buy a single ETF that perfectly mimics your benchmark (usually). But then, the underlying asset allocation will *still* be fluid as sectors and categories trade leadership.

Passive Is Hard . . . Really Hard. Some readers might find it hard to believe so many investors badly lag the market as passive investing seems so easy. But that's the problem—passive isn't easy. Done right (which many investors don't), it's very, very hard. That is exactly why investors lag.

To do passive right, first, you must believe with your heart and soul and very DNA (as I do) that capitalism is a great and powerful force for societal good. That the powers of human ingenuity and profit motive mean, long term, the world isn't doomed. That the opposite is true—that future innovations will be more than equal to smack down or at least greatly mitigate the challenges facing humanity. And you must believe earnings will keep rising in irregular fashion over time—hence, stocks will keep rising in irregular fashion over time.

What's more, you must have ice water in your veins. Passive investors would have had to sit through big bear markets like 2000–2002 and 2007–2009. The 2020 lightning-quick plunge, too. And 2022's nearly year-long slump. They'd have had to accept downward volatility—even huge volatility—as normal. And though painful, near-term losses eventually get wiped away by future and bigger upward volatility (yes, volatility goes both ways). They had to not panic and sell. They had to resist reallocating to categories they deemed "safe" at the time.

Remember, *products* like index funds may be passive in that their individual constituents mirror an underlying index. But if you buy and sell those funds, you aren't using them passively! If you mix and match various index funds in arbitrary weights (10% to small cap, 20% to "foreign," etc.), you are not passive. You are actively deviating from the overall market.

Truly passive long-term investors must believe with every fiber that portfolio declines—even huge ones—over relatively short periods like a year or even a few years won't damage their long-term results.

That's hard enough to do—mentally and emotionally. But equally as hard, they must calmly sit through periods when the market is up big—satisfied with just matching the benchmark. They must not get carried away by massive returns in a hot category and must not try to capture some excess return there.

They must simply be passive and believe, long term, stocks are likely to continue delivering superior returns at a premium over other similarly liquid asset classes. They can't tinker. They can't freak out. They can't in-and-out every three or so years as average mutual fund investors have done (as discussed in Chapter 2). And I've been in this business long enough and have studied behavioral finance enough to know that's a very, very tough thing for many investors to do.

With that, we're ready to delve in more depth into the determinants for benchmark selection, starting with time horizon.

Recap

Before deciding on asset allocation or making any other investment decisions, picking an appropriate benchmark is critical. Primary determinants for benchmark include:

- Return expectations
- Cash flow needs
- Time horizon
- Other personal factors, like security restrictions, personal preferences, etc.

Many posit asset allocation decisions are easily made simply by considering one's age and nothing else. This cookie-cutter approach ignores myriad personal factors that should figure into benchmark selection.

While a benchmark (and long-term asset allocation) shouldn't change much, if at all, tactical asset allocation can be (and often should be) much more flexible.

CHAPTER 4

Time Horizon—Longer Than You Think

In selecting a proper benchmark (the core of your retirement investing plan, driving all later investment decisions), your first stop is *time horizon.*

One of the bigger mistakes investors can make is underestimating time horizon—or having a fuzzy or ill-defined one. It can lead to major errors—ones that may not be evident immediately and maybe not for many years. Those can be the most insidious kinds of errors.

Most of the time, the errors stem not from mistakenly having *too long* a time horizon but *too short.* By not correctly assessing time horizon, investors might, for example, underestimate how much growth is needed to reach other goals, which they might not realize for 10 or 20 years. At that point, it could be too late to make a material enough shift to rectify it. Or your time horizon 20 years later might indeed be much shorter, which means a different benchmark is right for you. Either way, the damage may already be done.

In this chapter, we'll cover:

- Why ignoring opportunity cost can be perilous
- What exactly time horizon is (Hint: It likely *isn't* how long it is until you retire.)
- The effect time horizon has on your benchmark

Potential Pitfall: Ignoring Opportunity Cost

In the investing world, professionals, pundits, investors—almost everyone—often talk about *risk* when they mean *volatility*. The two are often interchangeable—and should be! But not always. Make no mistake, volatility is a key risk every investor faces and must consider, unless you're doing true, long-term capital preservation, which likely isn't the case for most readers of this book.

But it isn't the only risk! Thinking only or primarily about volatility can result in decisions that decrease the likelihood of reaching your long-term goals. For example, there's reinvestment risk—the risk interest rates fall, and when a bond matures, comparable bonds have lower (maybe much lower) coupon rates. Hence, you reinvest into a lower rate. There's inflation risk (covered in Chapter 2). There's political risk, interest rate risk, liquidity risk—myriad kinds of risk.

In 1997, I wrote a paper on risk with my friend and sometime research collaborator Meir Statman (the Glenn Klimek Professor of Finance at Santa Clara University's Leavey School of Business) titled "The Mean–Variance-Optimization Puzzle: Security Portfolios and Food Portfolios," which was published in the *Financial Analysts Journal.*

In it, we found how people think about food often parallels how investors think about investing. Diners don't just want nutrition—they want it to look good and taste good. And they want to eat the food at the right time of day—people feel weird eating hamburgers in the morning, and eating waffles at night is seen as quirky. And they want prestige! They don't want to look like a weirdo when their companion orders waffles at night in a fancy restaurant. And what people want shifts—often fast! What they feel as risk is what they want at a point in time that they think (or fear) they're not getting. They don't think about the things they *are* getting.

How does that relate to investing? You might hear investors say something like "I don't want any downside!" They're feeling negative volatility and want protection from it. Then, if stocks go on a long, sustained tear, they might feel like they're missing out—and *missing out* is felt as another kind of risk. That's the idea that what someone isn't getting at that point (downside protection, upside return, etc.) is what they're most concerned about—never mind if their other objectives are being met.

And a big risk investors often forget about—one that is particularly key when thinking about time horizon—is *opportunity cost*: the risk of giving up returns you would have otherwise gotten. If you assume a too-short time horizon and select a benchmark that may not be right for you, you may not have enough exposure to equities. And over your actual (and longer) time horizon, you may find the return you get is insufficient to allow you to get the cash flow you need, suitably outpace inflation, and/or grow your assets enough to accomplish all of your goals.

Again, volatility risk is a key risk and one that folks tend to feel most keenly, at least in the near term. It can be heart-stopping to watch your equity allocation—whether it's 100% of your portfolio or just 10%—lose 20% in value fast, as can happen in a correction. And even more grinding to watch it fall 30%, 40%, or more in a big bear market. Ultimately, equity investors put up with volatility because finance theory says (and history has supported), long term, you should get rewarded for that volatility—more so than in other, less volatile asset classes.

But focusing solely or primarily on volatility risk—thinking just about the lack of volatility that you want but aren't getting at a point in time—and ignoring opportunity cost can be very, well, costly. What's more, making up for lost opportunity can be very difficult. Investors may simply have to swallow a lower projected cash flow, lower expected returns, etc.

That can be hard to do, even dispiriting, if you've been counting on a larger income—particularly if you're already retired or nearing retirement—more so if your spouse was also counting on that income. (Try explaining that.) Or you could work longer to expand your portfolio size—also hard on you and the spouse. These are all tough realities to deal with—and you're likelier to avoid them if you don't underestimate your time horizon.

Time Horizon: What Is It?

Understanding what a proper time horizon is ties into my Chapter 1 point that people often think about their investing future in chopped-up phases. Investors often believe they have one time horizon that ends when they retire or start taking cash flow or hit some other milestone. Then they enter a new phase. Many investors think this way: "I'm 55. I plan to retire at 65. That means I have a 10-year time horizon." In my view, this is harmful thinking that potentially cuts you off at the knees.

Rather, your time horizon is how long you need your assets to work toward your objectives. For most retirement investors, this is their entire lives. If you don't want to risk the ire of your spouse and prefer they remember you fondly (and not with crass epithets), include their lifetime, too—particularly if your spouse is younger and/or healthier.

Figure 4.1 is a good start in thinking about time horizon. It's basic US life expectancy, produced by the Social Security

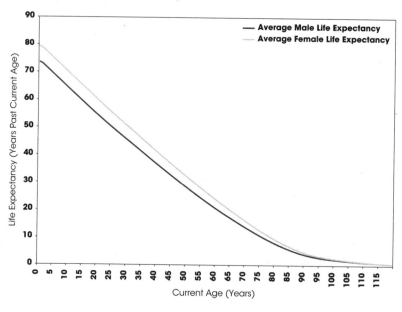

Figure 4.1 Life expectancy keeps getting longer
Source: Social Security Administration, as of 11/7/2024.

Administration. The *x*-axis shows current age, and the *y*-axis shows average life expectancy. So if you're 30, average life expectancy is another approximately 45 years if you're a man and 50 years if you're a woman (i.e., you could expect to live to 75 or 80 years old, respectively). If you're 70, average life expectancy is another approximately 14 years if you're a man and 17 years if you're a woman (implying total lifespans of 84 and 87 years).

And keep in mind, this is *average* life expectancy. Will you be average? Or above or below? There's no way to know with certainty. But a good way to estimate is considering the age your grandparents and parents died—as long as they died of natural causes. A car wreck at a young age is a tragedy but likely won't affect any genetic predisposition to longevity. If your grandparents died in their 80s and your parents are alive in their 90s, odds are good you'll live at least that long or longer, Social Security tables be damned. Then, consider your own health—perhaps high cholesterol runs in your family, but you diet and exercise and keep it under control. Your better health should, theoretically, add to your longevity.

Life Expectancy: Keeps Getting Longer

You want to err a bit on the longer side for a few reasons. First, you don't want to presume you'll live until 85, plan for your assets to last until then and no longer, and end up living into your 90s (as my parents did—it's very easy for me to envision long time horizons). Then, too, there are many comforts money can buy as you get older. (And don't forget the grandparent effect. Spoiling your grandkids is so darn fun—something I wouldn't have realized until I became a grandparent myself.)

But perhaps more important, average life expectancy has generally kept climbing. In 1900, men born in America had a life expectancy of just 46.4 years. Women's was 49.0—longer, but still crummy.[1]

Along came penicillin (discovered in 1928 and put into heavy rotation thereafter), and American males and females born in 1950 could expect to live to 65.6 and 71.1, respectively.[2] Add in the polio vaccine, the MMR vaccine, better screening for cancers and heart disease, new pharmaceuticals, and myriad other life-extending miracles, and US life expectancy through 2021—the latest data available—was 73.5 years for men and 79.3 years for women.[3] And that includes a tiny COVID-era dip. Life expectancies globally are extending, too—in Emerging Markets faster, but starting from a lower base.

Life expectancies likely only keep increasing. Loss of mobility can be a major factor in shortening life expectancy. Our hearts rely on mobility to help pump blood—if you aren't moving, your heart naturally wants to stop pumping so healthily. Just think of all the innovations in recent years—not just for older folks but for anyone with a loss of mobility. We've seen huge gains in prosthetics. In 2019, disabled American runner Blake Leeper finished fifth in the 400 meter at the USA Track & Field Outdoor Championships running on carbon fiber "blades."[4] They were so effective that officials barred him from competing in the Olympics, claiming the blades gave Leeper an unfair advantage![5]

More recently, researchers from MIT and Brigham and Women's Hospital found a way to let patients' own nervous systems—not robotic sensors—control their prosthetics.[6] Amazing! As this and other technologies mature, they naturally become more readily available and prices fall (as they always do when technologies mature). And they allow folks who would, not long ago, be immobile, to live much fuller, healthier, longer lives.

Innovation breeds future innovation, and there's no chance humanity wakes up tomorrow and decides "To hell with profits! And to hell with problem solving!" Never underestimate the power of profit motive in driving life-changing and life-extending innovations (that, combined with the desire to keep up with the grandkids for a little longer). Say you're 50 now, for example, and your average life expectancy (according to Social Security) is another 28 years (for men) or 32 years (for women). What are the odds, 30 years later, life expectancy has extended still more? Probably pretty good.

Shorter . . . and Longer

My view is folks tend to underestimate time horizons much more often than overestimate. But is it possible someone could have a shorter time horizon than their life expectancy? Of course! It can happen that an investor may have a set of circumstances making the time horizon shorter. But generally, for most investors, life expectancy can be a good jumping-off point to consider time horizon.

Can you have a time horizon much longer than an individual's or couple's life expectancy? Certainly. Many institutional investors—like college endowments, charities, pension funds, etc.—have literally an infinite time horizon. They aren't investing (often) for this life but for the long life they hope the endowment (charity, pension, etc.) has, which can stretch on for decades or even centuries, in many cases.

For individuals, super-long time horizons like that are unusual. However, many investors say, "This money isn't for me or my spouse. This is for the kids or grandkids or the Save the Piping Plover Foundation or some combination of the grandkids and plovers." In that case, the time horizon can indeed get pretty long—longer than your life expectancy.

Some readers may have a hard time thinking about a longer time horizon. Maybe they say, "I get it. I don't need cash flow now. But I need it in 10 years, and that's a big change. So shouldn't I think about the next 10 years one way and the following set of years another?"

Again, for most readers of this book, this is why *all* investing is retirement investing (usually). Your time horizon shouldn't be chopped into neat (or, heck, messy) segments. You shouldn't invest one way for this set of years and then radically change everything once you hit a milestone, just because you hit said milestone.

Whether you started investing today, 5 years ago, or 37 years ago and whether you're 22 or 35 or 57, your retirement investing plan should be crafted with an eye to your long-term goals, whether that means you plan on taking cash flow in 5, 10, or 50 years ... or never.

Now, maybe your milestone necessitates a change—a shift in benchmarks—maybe not. As discussed in Chapter 1, that change (big or small) may need to come 5 years in advance of that milestone or 7.2 years in advance or 4.6 years after. But those decisions should all be driven not by your retirement party date or the first distribution you take from your portfolio but by a long-term, forward-looking (always) assessment of what's needed for you to increase the likelihood you achieve your goals the entirety of the period you need your money working for you. If someone says to you "I retire in five years, and after that, I'll need to make a big change," your response should be "Why are you investing without a long-term plan?"

Time Horizon and Benchmark

Why the heck is time horizon so important? Generally, the longer the time horizon, the more a bigger allocation of equities becomes sensible in your benchmark.

This isn't to say time horizon is the only deciding factor. No! That would be akin to saying age is the only factor. But it is key. It must be considered alongside and in concert with return expectations, cash flow needs, and other factors. But a longer time horizon means investors have more time to grow beyond near-term equity volatility.

A fact that shocks no readers: Over short time periods, equities are generally more volatile than bonds. Figure 4.2 shows standard deviation (a common measure for volatility) and average annual rates of return over five-year rolling periods for a 100% equity allocation, a 70% equity/30% fixed income, a 50/50, and a 100% fixed-income allocation.

Measuring Volatility: Standard Deviation

One common way to measure volatility is *standard deviation*. It sounds fancy but is just what it sounds like—a measure of how much something deviates from its expected return. It can be used to measure historical volatility of single stocks, sectors, other categories, or the market as a whole. You can measure standard deviation for anything that has enough data points.

A low standard deviation means results didn't vary much from the average—i.e., low volatility. A higher number means there was more variability. Hence, over shorter periods, stocks have historically had a higher average standard deviation than fixed income.

An important point: Standard deviation always measures historic data and is therefore *backward looking*. It's useful, but not perfectly predictive.

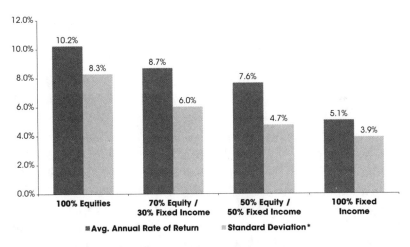

Figure 4.2 Five-year time horizon: volatility

Source: Finaeon, Inc., as of 2/21/2024. US 10-Year Government Bond Index, S&P 500 Total Return Index, average rate of return for rolling 5-year periods, 12/31/1925–12/31/2023. *Standard deviation represents the degree of fluctuations in historical returns. This risk measure is applied to five-year annualized rolling returns in the chart.

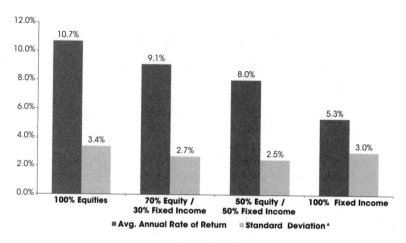

Figure 4.3 20-year time horizon: volatility
Source: Finaeon, Inc., as of 2/21/2024. US 10-Year Government Bond Index, S&P 500 Total Return Index, average rate of return for rolling 20-year periods, 12/31/1925–12/31/2023. *Standard deviation represents the degree of fluctuations in historical returns. This risk measure is applied to 20-year annualized rolling returns in the chart.

Equities have a superior return over five-year periods—the 100% equity allocation averages 10.2%—but with much higher standard deviation. And as the share of equities decreases, so does the standard deviation. The 100% fixed-income allocation has the lowest average annual return at 5.1%. But it also has the lowest standard deviation. Less wiggling means lower returns. Pretty straightforward.

But if you look at longer periods, something happens. Figure 4.3 shows standard deviation and average annual returns, but over 20-year rolling periods. Standard deviation for 100% equities is much lower over 20 years than over 5 years. And over 20 years, average standard deviation for 100% equities and 100% fixed income are quite close—3.4% versus 3.0%.

Figure 4.4 shows 30-year rolling periods. Over 30 years, the average standard deviation for 100% equities is actually *lower*

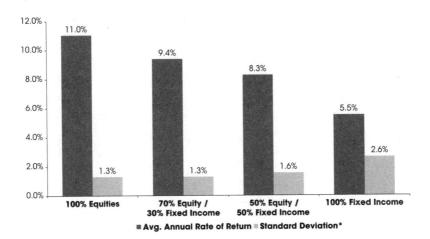

Figure 4.4 30-year time horizon: volatility

Source: Finaeon, Inc., as of 2/21/2024. US 10-Year Government Bond Index, S&P 500 Total Return Index, average rate of return for rolling 30-year periods, 12/31/1925–12/31/2023. *Standard deviation represents the degree of fluctuations in historical returns. This risk measure is applied to 30-year annualized rolling returns in the chart.

than for 100% fixed income—1.3% for equities versus 2.6% for fixed income. Lower standard deviation with materially better long-term average annual returns.

Day to day, month to month, and year to year over those 20- and 30-year periods, equities swung much more wildly than fixed income (as depicted in Figure 4.2). But the data show, over longer periods, the wild wiggles resolve to more consistent *upward* volatility. (Remember, volatility goes up, too.) Folks often think when stocks rise, that's good, but when they fall, that's volatility. But they're wrong. They're two sides to the same coin, and you don't get big returns without volatility—up *and* down.

Said another way, volatility is normal. Bear markets are normal. They happen. Sometimes they're big. But if you're an investor with a 20-year time horizon or more, even a big bear market like 2008's likely becomes a blip after several decades of equity-like growth. Near-term vicissitudes simply get swamped by the later, longer, and stronger overall upsweep of equity markets—history shows that.

Now, if you believe "this time, it's different" and, in the future, equities aren't likely to continue delivering superior returns relative to similarly liquid asset classes, I direct you to my 2011 book, *Markets Never Forget*. Investors nearly always believe "this time, it's different"—that phrasing pops up repeatedly through history and can be tracked in media. But "this time" isn't ever all that different as folks fear. Yes, details differ and the scenery changes, but humans don't evolve fast enough to make our behaviors change. And markets reflect the behavior of billions of people doing trillions of transactions daily.

There have always been and always will be contractions and bear markets. There will always be outsized fear the future is doomed—particularly following recessions and bear markets (sometimes for *years* after). But the future won't be doomed—economies will keep rising in fits and starts, and, very likely, equity markets will keep notching new highs, given enough time.

This doesn't necessarily mean an equity strategy is a fit for all investors because that will depend on a number of considerations. Rather, this highlights why determining the correct time horizon is critical for your benchmark and your retirement investing plan.

Recap

Time horizon is among the primary determinants of a proper benchmark. It's critical you understand what it is and what it is not.

Time horizon is not: How long it is until you retire, how long it is until you plan to start taking cash flow, or how long it is until you reach some other milestone.

Time horizon is: How long you want your assets to work for you—often your entire life and that of your spouse. Maybe a bit longer if you want to pass a chunk to the kids or grandkids. And don't forget:

- Average life expectancy is just that—an average. Half will live longer.
- Life expectancies keep expanding.
- *Don't forget to account for your spouse*—particularly if they are younger/healthier.

And don't forget—volatility is just one type of risk investors face. *Opportunity cost* is a very real and often costly risk—the risk of doing something now that may cheat you of superior returns down the road.

CHAPTER 5

What's in a Return?

Once you've got your timeline nailed down, another key consideration for selecting a proper benchmark is your return expectations. This links directly to your growth goal—but also your cash flow goal.

Many readers may say, "Sure, I want growth. Who doesn't?" But they may underestimate how much growth is necessary for their goals. They may forget to account for inflation's impact. Or they may fail to plan for later unexpected events or underestimate how much cash flow they'll need. As in determining the time horizon, errors here are much more often made by assuming the need for too little growth, not too much.

Investors may also not understand what level of growth is reasonably possible. Or, what level of volatility they should expect for that amount of growth. Misunderstanding what amount of growth is reasonable to expect and the volatility risk involved can also lead to errors. (The worst of which, in my view, is falling prey to a scam. Sometimes, the return *of* your money is more important than the return *on* your money.)

Then, some readers may think they have only modest growth goals. All they need is a small amount (or, heck, a large amount) of cash flow from their portfolio. They care not one whit about whether the portfolio value grows, shrinks, or depletes. The last check can bounce! However, as discussed in Chapter 2, if you want cash flow—even if you don't want to grow your portfolio a bunch—that often necessitates some growth to stretch the portfolio, particularly when you consider inflation's impact on later purchasing power ... and the fact longer life expectancies mean you don't know which check is the last very far in advance (if you even still *use* checks).

Clearly defining your growth goal so you can have reasonable return expectations is critical to increasing the odds of long-term success. Why? An example: Often investors have as a goal being "safe." This might be expressed like "I want to keep my investments safe. So I'll invest in mostly cash and bonds and avoid volatility, and that will keep me safe."

And maybe a non-volatile strategy like that will! Keep in mind, as mentioned elsewhere, bonds can and do lose value in the near term—even Treasurys—and if you must liquidate, you can liquidate at a loss. If you sold bonds in 2022, you know that all too well.

But "safe" is a nebulous term. There's no technical definition of it, and what safety means to one person might mean something totally different to another (like our opportunity cost discussion in Chapter 4)—and you want to be as clear as possible about your goals.

Rather than "safe"—which is hard to define and means varying things to varying people—I prefer you think about whether a particular strategy is right for you. And whether a strategy that eliminates most or all volatility is right for you or not depends on your long-term goals and other personal considerations. If your long-term goals require growth, eliminating volatility and routinely holding mostly cash and fixed income likely reduces your long-term returns (maybe by a lot). You may think the lack of volatility feels okay now—but you may not feel so great 10, 20, 30 years from now. Long term, you may have seriously reduced the odds you achieve your goals. And that could make you feel much less safe years down the road because your strategy is off target.

This chapter will cover:

- How to think about growth
- How to set reasonable return expectations
- Why the past is a useful (though imperfect) guide
- Why having unrealistic expectations can be very, very dangerous

Growth Defined

What exactly is "growth"? It might seem clear-cut, but there are myriad return objectives that can be considered growth. And there are myriad degrees of growth on the growth spectrum.

On one end of the spectrum is market-like growth. Historically, the long-term average for stocks has been about 10% annualized.[1] And in my view, odds are stocks continue delivering about that over very long periods ahead—maybe a bit more, maybe a bit less. Again, remember: To get to that long-term equity average, whether stocks are 10% of your benchmark or 100%, **the equity portion will experience near-term volatility**—often huge. It's the *long term* that historically has gotten stocks to higher average annualized returns over other similarly liquid asset classes.

Can you net more than that? Sure! If using stocks, you can deviate from the benchmark and aim to beat the market. As discussed in Chapter 3, you needn't always be right, just right more than wrong on average over a long period. This is very hard to do over long periods, and few professional money managers have done it—but it is possible.

Can you net *materially* more than that? Again, it is possible in theory, but you'd need to take on *materially more* than market-like risk and be fairly consistently right, which is very hard to do. For example, a way to get mega-outsized returns would be to concentrate heavily—in just a few stocks or maybe a few narrow categories. If you're right—and right repeatedly and for a long time—returns can be huge. If you can do that successfully, first, you're exceedingly unique. No professional money manager I'm aware of has a long-term record beating the market using a strategy of holding just a few stocks or narrow categories.

There are money managers who do invest in narrow categories, but they go in and out of favor, usually, with their category—sometimes beating the market, sometimes lagging by a lot. And some individual investors no doubt have been exceedingly lucky with a narrow selection of stocks—emphasis on *exceedingly lucky*. But on average, that isn't a proven market-beating strategy. However, if this is you and you have done this and can do this in the future, you don't need this book anyway. For other readers, you likely don't want your retirement plans to hinge on something that is an exceedingly low probability.

Is it possible to get bigger returns another way? Absolutely. Take your cash and start a successful business. As I wrote in my 2008 book, *The Ten Roads to Riches,* founding a successful business is a way to make mega-bucks. It's risky—very risky—but the payoff can be huge.

Most of the richest of the rich got that way as founder-CEOs. Bill Gates. Larry Ellison. Elon Musk. Sam Walton's founder-CEO wealth was so massive that, even split among his children and heirs, several of them rank among the top 20 in the *Forbes* 400 list of richest Americans.[2] Jeff Bezos. Mark Zuckerberg. Sergey Brin. Larry Page. Michael Dell. Alice Walton is the richest American woman, behind only L'Oreal heiress and Chairwoman Francoise Bettencourt Meyers globally. All these people made their wealth (or owe much of their wealth—which the Waltons have added to) to founder-CEO riches.[3] But that's not just an investment plan, it's also a career choice—one in which you likely fail at least a few times before hitting success, if you ever do.

The marvelous thing about the entrepreneurial road to riches is, done right, you *should* fail. You will fail. But you can and should dust yourself off and try again. (Folks who don't succeed on this road often don't dust off and try again.) The biggest successes on the *Forbes* 400 (and the *Forbes* billionaire list, for that matter) didn't see success right out of the gate. They tried and blew up—often multiple times—and still acquired massive wealth. It's an incredibly trying road but, ultimately, a very rewarding one. But for that, you need a different book.

Another way to get outsize returns: You could invest in raw land or develop high rises or shopping malls. Those, too, are very risky paths. And this also isn't the book for you. (But, again, you could read Chapter 9 in *The Ten Roads to Riches* on being a land baron—which also is more of a career choice than a retirement investing plan.)

However, in general, my recommendation to folks thinking about a long-term investment plan, who already have day jobs or are currently in retirement (and who believe in the power of capitalism), is to stick to relatively liquid assets, like stocks, bonds, cash, and/or other securities.

At the other end of the growth scale, you might state your goal as "I want to just keep pace with inflation"—doing a little bit better than cash. Maybe you aren't taking cash flows and you want to maintain your portfolio's current value after inflation. You aren't aiming for huge returns, but stashing your cash under the mattress won't work unless moving forward over your long time horizon, inflation stays flat (unlikely), or we have prolonged deflation (which you really don't want—symptomatic of other bigger problems). Just to keep pace with inflation requires some growth.

In between are varying magnitudes. For example: You want to target some dollar amount, as in "I have $1 million now. In 30 years, I want to leave $4 million to my favorite charity."

Or maybe you have a cash flow goal. If you do, you may need your portfolio to stretch to varying degrees to cover that. How much growth will depend on how much cash flow you need, what the cash flow is for (discretionary or nondiscretionary expenses—or both), and which goal is more important to you—growth or cash flow. Or maybe you think they're equally important.

For example, you may care mostly (or entirely) about cash flow—let the last check bounce, as they say—and think you needn't worry about your portfolio's return at all. Can you stick it all in laddered Treasurys—which will reduce volatility but might not outpace inflation? Maybe. Maybe not. If your portfolio isn't big enough to allow for straight-line depreciation, you probably do need some growth.

And don't forget about inflation. You may want (as an example) $50,000 from your portfolio annually. But to increase the likelihood your cash flows can keep pace with inflation and your purchasing power isn't eroded over time (as discussed in Chapter 4), you likely need growth. How much growth will depend on your time horizon, how big your portfolio is, how much cash flow you need, etc. (See how all of these considerations play into each other?) In general, when thinking about growth, it isn't unusual for investors to underestimate how much growth is needed for their long-term goals.

Expecting Volatility

If you have a longer time horizon and growth goals, then you need some equities in your benchmark. The more growth you need and the longer your time horizon, the bigger equity allocation you likely require. Unfortunately, there's no easy-to-follow prescriptive formula. Again, such things ignore the myriad factors unique to you. But as a general guide (and setting aside, for now, the impact of cash flows), the more equities you have in your benchmark, the higher your long-term growth prospects.

And the more equities you have, the more you'll be exposed to shorter-term downside volatility. But—I said this in Chapter 4, and I'll say it again—volatility is normal.

(One more time.) Volatility is normal, to be expected, and not a signal of long-term trouble. If you need growth, you need some degree of equities, and you will be exposed to volatility—both up and down. This is true of all asset classes. All asset classes experience price volatility. As you create your retirement investing plan, that must be part of what you expect, or you could be setting yourself up for mistakes—maybe hugely costly ones.

Why? Folks often run into trouble, not because their port-folios are suffering market-like downside (if they have a long time horizon). No—they often run into trouble because they suffer market-like downside and *then* panic and decide to bail on stocks or make some other major change. (In effect, buying high and selling low.) Material changes to your benchmark should be driven by (you know this cold now) time horizon, return expectations, cash flow needs, or some other major factor. They shouldn't be driven solely by the discomfort caused by near-term volatility.

Making such material changes—driven by fear, not something fundamental that's changed—is often what causes folks to badly lag the market on average (as discussed in Chapter 2). For many investors, it isn't the volatility that hurts them long term but their reaction to it.

The Past as a Guide?

So what's reasonable to expect? History can be a useful (though not infallible) guide in setting expectations. History and finance theory tell us that in the long term, increased volatility (done right) increases return.

Now, some may argue the past isn't a reasonable guide at all! That was then, and "it's different this time," and the world is some new, horrible place. We've entered into long-term decline, and stocks (bonds, too, for that matter) will never get anything close to their historic returns, and we should all stash gold bars in our backyards. So on and so forth.

First, I would say, if your outlook is so dire, forget gold. What you want is a rifle. And maybe a dairy cow and a tall fence. And reread Chapter 4 (as well as my 2011 book, *Markets Never Forget*).

The past isn't predictive of the future. That stocks, bonds, cash, gold, real estate, pork bellies, baseball cards, and anything anyone buys and sells and believes has value did something in the past doesn't mean it must do the same thing in the future. However, investing is about probabilities, not certainties. In capital markets, there are no certainties. Rather, you can use the past to inform you if something is within the realm of reasonable to expect.

One example: Early in 2009, in the final days of steep bear market volatility, a bottom was forming. But few could see it for all the wild market swings, and many were fiercely fearful of stocks. Professionals and punditry spilled plenty of ink—all through 2009 and even years after—that the future was bleak and stocks were done, and for the long period ahead, bonds were likely to outperform stocks. They called it the "new normal." What followed? History's longest equity bull market, running nearly 11 years with stocks vastly outperforming bonds. Or, more succinctly, the old normal.

A similar panic came in March 2020, amid COVID lockdowns that walloped economic activity. Remember talk of forever-changed economies? The death of the travel industry? The end of office life? Even the swan song of handshakes and hugs? How could stocks ever thrive again? many wondered. Yet after that March's low, US stocks soared 70.2% through 2020's end—just as they soared off 2009's bottom. The specifics may have differed, but the overall pattern—fear of doom and then a huge relief rally—did not.

Now, were all those dire outcomes *possible*? Of course! It's possible stocks do lousy for a long period ahead. But just as investing is about probabilities, not certainties, it also isn't about *possibilities*. There are infinite possibilities—if you spent your life thinking about them, you wouldn't get out of bed in the morning, much less buy a stock thinking of your financial life 20 years out.

To make a proper retirement plan, you want to start thinking in the realm of probabilities. For example, is it possible stocks do lousy over the long period ahead—10 or 20 or 30 years—thereby rendering your expectations hugely wide of the mark?

Sure!

Is it probable? Let's consider. Table 5.1 shows the historical frequency of positive returns for stocks. On a daily basis, stocks are positive 53% of the time—a little better than a coin flip. And negative days can come in clumps—that can be what contributes to feeling like stocks aren't positive all that darn much. Now, positive days come in clumps, too, but it's human nature to fear losses more than we look forward to gains, so our minds misremember the positive clumps. The negative clumps just loom larger in our brains, even if that isn't what reality is.

Calendar months are positive 62.9% of the time historically, 68.9% of quarters are positive, and 73.5% of calendar years are up. Rolling 12-months are positive slightly more than calendar years, which makes sense—a calendar year is a wholly arbitrary set of 12 months. Rolling 10-year periods are positive a big 94.5% of the time—making such events high probabilities going forward. No rolling 20-year period has ever been negative, making a negative 20-year a very low probability.

Figure 5.1 is another good demonstration of the data in Table 5.1. It shows the historic probability of positive returns versus your holding period hits 70% at 4 months, 80% at about 1.5 years, 90% around 5.5 years, and 100% around 15.5 years. Not so shabby. It also tells you something about fears of shorter-term stock volatility. If you can force yourself to think just a bit longer-term, fears of downside volatility should start to abate. If, for example, you could take a pill that made you forget about your portfolio except for once every five years, when you check in, odds are stocks will be up. Odds are supremely good if you take the 10-year pill! (This also underscores the importance of picking a proper benchmark.) The longer you give stocks, the more that shorter-term downside volatility resolves historically to more consistent and bigger upside volatility.

Table 5.1   Stocks' Historical Frequency of Positive Returns

S&P 500 Returns (As of 12/31/2023)					
	Number of Periods			Percent of Periods	
	Positive	Negative	Total	Positive	Negative
Daily Returns*	13,157	11,610	24,767	53.1%	46.9%
Calendar Month Returns	739	436	1,175	62.9%	37.1%
Calendar Quarter Returns	270	122	392	68.9%	31.1%
Calendar Year Returns	72	26	98	73.5%	26.5%
Rolling 1 Year Returns, Monthly	873	291	1,164	75.0%	25.0%
Rolling 5 Year Returns, Monthly	986	130	1,116	88.4%	11.6%
Rolling 10 Year Returns, Monthly	998	58	1,056	94.5%	5.5%
Rolling 20 Year Returns, Monthly	936	0	936	100.0%	0.0%
Rolling 25 Year Returns, Monthly	876	0	876	100.0%	0.0%

*Daily return data begins 1/1/1928 and is based on price appreciation only; all other data begins 1/31/1926 and reflect total return.
Source: Finaeon, Inc.; as of 2/23/2024. S&P 500 Total Return Index from 1/31/1926 to 12/31/2023.

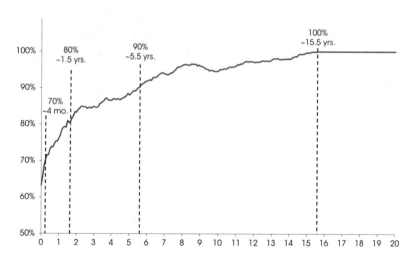

Figure 5.1 The historic probability of positive returns versus holding period
Source: Finaeon, Inc., as of 4/11/2024. Calculated using monthly rolling holding periods, 1/31/1926–12/31/2023.

These data show that fears bad stretches will breed more bad stretches are bunk. When I wrote the first edition of this book in 2012, many posited that the 2000s' nearly flat full-decade returns meant something was fundamentally awry—so the 2010s were likelier to be lousy.

It's true that returns were pretty lousy overall during the 2000s—US stocks annualized −0.95% and world stocks −0.24% (a cumulative −9.10% and −2.41%).[4] However, my view is 10 years is as arbitrary as any other period to measure stocks. Keep in mind, too, the two biggest bear markets since the Great Depression by magnitude bookended the decade. That stock returns still managed to be about flat is pretty remarkable and speaks volumes about the overall resilience of capital markets.

But does an overall flat or down period portend a future flat or down period? Does it increase the probability of future lousiness? To make that argument, you'd need to find evidence that, overwhelmingly, past flat or down 10-year periods led to the same in the future.

I find none. First of all, flat or down 10-year periods are pretty rare. (As Table 5.1 showed, rolling 10-year periods are positive 94.5% of the time.) What's more, in every 10-year rolling period (measured monthly using the longer history of US stocks) for which I could measure a subsequent 10-year rolling period, *every subsequent 10-year period was positive.*[5] Not just positive—hugely positive! The worst 10-year return following a flat-to-down 10-year period was 98.6%—i.e., stocks doubled.[6] That was the worst one! The 2010s market malaise that so many predicted? US stocks skyrocketed 256.7%![7] There's just no evidence a negative 10-year period has historically led to a lousy 10-year period ahead—making future such events low probabilities.

Figures 5.2 through 5.6 show some notable 10-year periods of down or flat US stock returns and the returns in the subsequent 10 years. Note, the first "lousy" 10 years were never uniformly lousy. They often featured periods of big upside volatility. And the subsequent 10 years, though overall great, also featured a lot of shorter-term volatility. That's just how markets work.

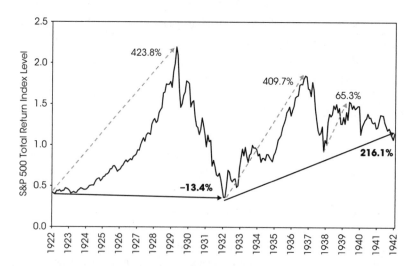

Figure 5.2 Negative 10, positive 10—1922 to 1942

Source: Finaeon, Inc., as of 8/15/2011. S&P 500 Total Return Index, 5/31/1922–5/31/1942.

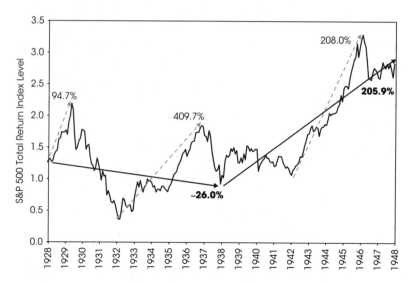

Figure 5.3 Negative 10, positive 10—1928 to 1948

Source: Finaeon, Inc., as of 8/15/2011. S&P 500 Total Return Index, 3/31/1928–3/31/1948.

Figure 5.4 Negative 10, positive 10—1929 to 1949

Source: Finaeon, Inc., as of 8/15/2011. S&P 500 Total Return Index, 8/31/1929–8/31/1949.

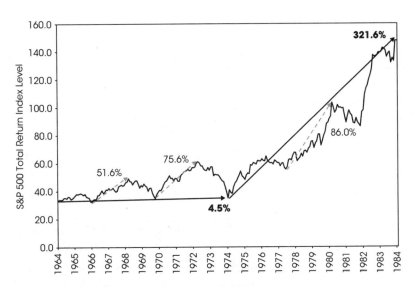

Figure 5.5 Flat 10, positive 10—1964 to 1984

Source: Finaeon, Inc., as of 8/15/2011. S&P 500 Total Return Index, 9/30/1964–9/30/1984.

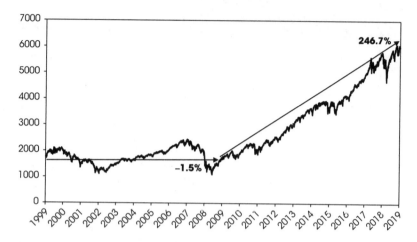

Figure 5.6 Flat 10, positive 10—1999 to 2019
Source: Finaeon, Inc., as of 11/4/2024. S&P 500 Total Return Index, 9/30/1999–9/30/2019.

Does all of this mean something that has never happened can't happen? No! The weird and wacky are always possibilities. But remember, investing is about considering probabilities, not trying to outmaneuver every possibility.

Stocks Beat Bonds—Usually

Stocks are typically positive over longer periods—history shows that. What's more, over longer periods, they also typically outperform bonds.

There have been 79 rolling 20-year periods (measuring full calendar years) since 1926. In 77 of them (97.5% of occurrences), stocks outperformed bonds.[8] Over 20 years, stocks returned an average 806% and bonds 232%—stocks beat bonds by a 3.5-to-1 margin.[9] In the rare examples when bonds beat stocks, it was by just a 1.1-to-1 margin—and stocks were still positive, averaging 239% to bonds' 257%.[10] Little reward for a move that rarely worked—not the way you think a rare payout should work.

Over 30-year rolling periods, bonds have never beaten stocks. Stocks returned an average 2,359% (compounding growth is awesome!) to bonds' 547%—a 4.3-to-1 margin.[11]

This isn't to say bonds are a bad investment or not right for you. They may very well be part of a proper benchmark for you. But the function of bonds in a benchmark is often to reduce overall volatility, not increase future expected return. Further, the aim here is to help you set reasonable expectations for not only returns but the degree of volatility likely necessary for that return.

Forecasting for Future Supply?

So stocks are typically positive over long periods and typically beat bonds, historically. Yet, it's periodically popular to predict a looming "lost decade" ahead—in which stocks do lousy overall and/or lag bonds. We know, now, such an event is a low probability—and perhaps even a lower probability following a period when stocks were indeed flat or even down.

That doesn't mean it can't happen! But for a prediction for a low-probability event to hold more weight—for something like another lousy 10 years of stock returns to follow a flat (or down) 10 years—there would need to be some reason, rooted in fundamentals and/or finance theory, increasing the likelihood. And it would have to be something few people currently appreciate: What moves stocks are underappreciated or misunderstood fundamental factors—not things splashed across the front page of newspapers, especially not repeats.

Nor should the reason be "it's different this time" because people always think it's different this time, and it almost never is. (Sir John Templeton famously said, "The four most expensive words in the English language are, 'This time it's different.'") And it can't be that we've *been* through a tough time—recession, credit crisis, big bear market, even a pandemic—because that's backward looking, not forward looking, and stocks are, always and everywhere, forward looking.

Finally, and as important, no one ever in the history of capital markets forecasting has successfully and repeatedly made long-term forecasts—i.e., where stocks are going over the next 5, 7, 10 years. And if they did once or twice, it was purely by coincidence. Why?

Stock prices are determined (like everything else) by supply and demand. In the very near term, supply is relatively fixed—it takes time and effort and a lot of forewarning for new firms to enter the market (via an initial public offering [IPO]). The same holds true when they do subsequent offerings, which add to stock supply. Firms can also go bankrupt or do cash-based mergers and acquisitions (M&A)—which reduce supply—but M&A still doesn't happen overnight, and bankruptcies don't happen enough to make a big dent in near-term supply.

So, over the next 12–24 months, supply doesn't affect prices much—demand does. But that changes over longer periods. Over longer periods, supply can expand or contract near infinitely and, therefore, has a much greater influence over prices. So to know where prices are likely to be 10 years from now, you must know something about stock supply direction eight and nine years from now, which is simply impossible to know now. Nor do I know of anyone even attempting to forecast far distant stock supply.

Hence, after a bad 10-year stretch, anyone telling you the next 10 years are likelier to be lousy because the last 10 years were flat or down is, first, simply saying they think immediate history will repeat—which isn't a great way to approach capital markets forecasting. Another way to think about that: Were the 2000s likelier to have outstanding, above-average equity returns because the 1990s did? No—of course not. Second, that person is telling you more about what they don't know about capital markets than what they do know. Unless, of course, they cracked how to accurately and repeatedly forecast future stock supply. In which case, I would appreciate it if that person would call me.

This means your best guide to knowing if something is reasonable to expect is history, combined with a good understanding of finance theory and a rational assessment of fundamentals and current market conditions. We have a long history of data for US stocks and many market cycles to consider. And the US stock market is sufficiently broad to serve as a good proxy for world stocks—for which we have a decent but not as long data history. Don't expect history to repeat exactly or to be predictive—but you can use it as a guide for shaping forward-looking probabilities.

Gordon Moore and Endless Innovation

One more thing on this topic before moving on. No one can tell you what stocks, bonds, commodities, anything will do in the long future ahead. That's part of the feature of taking risk to get return. If returns were certain, returns would likely be lower.

What's more, it shouldn't surprise you stocks are likelier to net better returns than bonds in the future—or any other similarly liquid asset class. Or gold or real estate (whose long-term returns have also both badly lagged stocks and likely will in the long-term future).

What is a stock? A stock is a piece of firm ownership. It's a slice of future earnings—you buy a stock because you expect future earnings to rise. Otherwise, why bother? But more important—stocks adapt. Stocks represent ownership of the collective world of business—the accumulated knowledge and experience of the world. They reflect the relatively constant onslaught of science and technology. When some new technology is created, those who benefit most aren't those who built the innovation, but those who learn how to use it and market it broadly to humanity—i.e., public stocks.

Bonds are fine! A bond is a promise to return your principal with interest. It isn't a piece of future earnings—it's debt.

A contract. You could actively trade bonds to increase your expected return—which increases the amount of risk you face (which is fine, as long as you understand what you're undertaking). They are subject to default and price volatility (like all asset classes). But the nature of debt—a contract between two people—doesn't change once the transaction takes place.

Gold doesn't adapt—it's a lump of metal with limited industrial use. Its returns are linked tightly to demand since supply of the hard asset increases at a slow, predictable rate. And demand can be fickle! But over time, gold doesn't change and adapt. Real estate either! It's largely leverage that can make some real estate returns outsized. What's more, folks often underestimate maintenance and other costs associated with real estate, which can be tough to tabulate and properly account for.

Only stocks represent the limitless bounds of human innovation—the irregular, herky-jerky march to increased earnings over time. And, in my view, humanity isn't nearly done innovating yet. Anyone who has ever bet against our ability to problem-solve has been proven wrong over time, again and again.

In 1798, Thomas Malthus infamously first predicted human population growth would soon outpace food production. He utterly rejected the idea of "unlimited progress" in food production. Seven billion more people later, there are some who still believe, *this time*, human ingenuity has peaked. (How they square that with all the myriad times people have thought that in the past and been wrong is beyond me. But never mind.)

I don't buy it. Neither should you. Here's why: Moore's Law. If you get in your bones the concept of Moore's Law, you know innovation isn't at an end. Moore's Law states the number of transistors that can fit on an integrated circuit should double every two years. Gordon Moore, the visionary co-founder of Intel, first conceived that in a paper in 1965. And that prediction was about spot-on—development of integrated circuits has about followed that pace.

But it wasn't just about integrated circuits. What Moore conceptualized was the endless and exponential upward sweep of innovation. That innovation will build upon innovation in perfectly unpredictable ways. Another way of thinking about that is, in 20 years, electronics as we know them today will cost about 5% of what they cost today but will be able to do vastly more. What that *more* is we just don't know yet.

Those who thought smartphones, smart TVs, tablets, and cloud computing represented some kind of pinnacle of innovation quickly found they were wrong—enter ChatGPT and artificial intelligence! And those who think AI is the caboose of the innovation train will be wrong, too. I don't know how precisely. But folks working on seemingly unrelated technologies in far-flung locations, unbeknownst to each other, will see their technologies collide in some way at some point they could never have conceived of when they made their creations. That's how new technologies happen. It can't be planned. (Politicians cannot and will never understand this—not in their nature—which is why central planning is always a disastrous way to run an economy.) It's an insanely chaotic, messy road to the next how-did-we-live-without-this invention.

Never underestimate humanity's ingenuity and ability to problem-solve. The world hasn't outgrown its ability to feed itself as Malthus thought. Building on past innovations, someone invented the steel plow, the tractor, the threshing machine, better fertilizers, and dwarf wheat. Handily, someone also discovered penicillin, the pasteurization process, and the polio vaccine, so we have a better shot at getting past age five. And then someone (again, building on myriad past inventions) invented smartphones, too, so we can live, not starve, and be entertained all the while. Malthus didn't think about smartphones any more than he thought about dwarf wheat or the MMR vaccine.

Hence, unless you believe humanity has altered so much that people are no longer motivated to innovate, problem-solve, and chase profits, then stocks should continue to be superior to all similarly liquid asset classes.

Potential Pitfall: Unrealistic Expectations

Throughout the book, I caution against unrealistic expectations. Why? Having unrealistic expectations or failing to plan for enough growth can expose investors to numerous risks, including falling prey to a con artist.

Ponzi schemers will get anyone they can—no one is immune. They want big investors but are more than delighted to steal from investors with smaller pools. To keep their scam going, they need a steady stream of money, no matter the source. And folks who want easy or big returns with little risk can be good marks for a Ponzi scamster. A con artist knows folks who think big gains are possible without much risk won't question them hard. Con artists hate being questioned hard.

One standard way these rats operate is how Bernie Madoff carried out his multibillion-dollar fraud. For years, his investors' statements (all dummied up, as it turns out) showed about 10% growth each year—give or take a bit.

That may not seem unusual. Except he wasn't claiming 10% *annualized* growth over a long period—which is about what stocks have done historically. His statements showed about 10–12% growth *each and every year* with little variability. Even monthly returns were eerily steady.

Such a thing is not only historically unprecedented (remember—history is a good guide for letting you know if something is reasonable to expect), but it also flies in the face of finance theory.

To get market-like returns on average, you must accept market-like volatility. A portfolio with returns matching long-term equity averages and effectively no year-to-year variability

Table 5.2   Average Returns Aren't Normal—Normal Returns Are Extreme

S&P 500 Annual Return Range	Occurrences Since 1926	Frequency	
> 40%	5	5.1%	Up a lot (37.8%
30% to 40%	15	15.3%	of the time)
20% to 30%	17	17.3%	
10% to 20%	21	21.4%	Up a little (35.7%
0% to 10%	14	14.3%	of the time)
−10% to 0%	13	13.3%	Down a little
−20% to −10%	7	7.1%	(20.4% of the time)
−30% to −20%	3	3.1%	Down a lot
−40% to −30%	2	2.0%	(6.1% of the time)
< −40%	1	1.0%	
Total Occurrences	98		
Simple Average	12.1%		
Annualized Average	10.3%		

Source: Finaeon, Inc., as of 3/25/2024. S&P 500 annual total returns.

should set off millions of red flags, flares, and rockets. Market-like returns with no variability is an investor's dream, but, as I wrote in my 2009 book, *How to Smell a Rat*, returns that seem too good to be true very often are. Dream becomes nightmare.

To get something like 10% annualized returns, an adviser should have years when returns are up much more than 10% and years when returns are down big. Full-year market returns are rarely close to 10%. They're much more wildly variable than that. Table 5.2 shows how often returns historically have been up a lot, up a little, down a little, and down a lot. Interestingly, the most common occurrence by a plurality (37.8% of the time) is stocks being up a lot. And you already know from Table 5.1 stocks are down just 26.5% of calendar years. But down years shouldn't be an absolute non-occurrence for a portfolio that annualizes about 10% over long periods.

If you expect close to long-term market average returns each and every year with little to no volatility, you could be setting yourself up to be a mark. Look for the big down years—that's proof a manager is likely an honest dealer.

Another common financial scam artist tactic is promising huge, pie-in-the-sky returns. *Much* above long-term equity averages. They might promise this in a stock (or other security) portfolio, or they might promise this for some other investment—real estate, new business start-up, currencies (the Iraqi dinar scam has long been a popular one), etc.

Recently, cryptocurrency scammers have promised huge returns to lure investors. The crypto fund HyperVerse offered "memberships" touting 0.5% returns *per day*—300% in less than two years![12] Who wouldn't want that? But the fund collapsed in 2022, leaving investors high and dry. The "CEO" who promoted it turned out not to exist—he was a paid actor, hired via an online intermediary.[13] The Securities and Exchange Commission charged the fund's founder and promoter with fraud, alleging they ran a $1.7 billion pyramid scheme.[14] If it looks too good to be true, it probably is.

Yes, it is possible to hugely outperform equity markets. Doing so consistently is very, very hard. And even managers who have long-term histories of outperforming markets on average *still* have years they lagged and *still* have years they were down big.

But outside yields on bank Certificate of Deposit and Treasurys, no one can promise you anything. (And if you sell either before they mature, you can experience a loss.) Even the bank CD has risk—if the bank goes belly up (it happens), the bank may not have additional protections above standard FDIC guarantees. Even annuities, which may guarantee an annual cash flow and/or return (depending on the contract), are only as good as the insurance firm is solvent. Insurance firms can and do fail. A promise to deliver a return from anyone besides the US government *should be considered a scam.*

Avoiding a Rat

In my 2009 book, *How to Smell a Rat*, I detailed five key signs of potential financial fraud. The biggest sign to look for: a manager who also has custody of your assets.

If a manager custodies the assets—i.e., makes all the decisions on what to buy and sell and when but *also* controls the entity where assets are housed—it is functionally nothing for them to dummy up statements and/or take your money out the back door.

In every financial Ponzi scheme I've studied, the manager always had direct access to the dough. Or, if they used a third-party custodian, they had some direct influence. If you insist on separation of decision-maker and custody (and that custodian is a major, big-name outfit with proper controls in place), it becomes nearly impossible for a manager to do a Ponzi.

Now, there are many legitimate reasons for an adviser to custody assets. But it does remove one major and additional layer of protection. When I set up my firm, I intentionally set it up so money managed for individual clients would be held elsewhere.

These are other key signs of financial fraud:

- Returns too good to be true.
- An investing strategy that is murky, flashy, or "too complicated" for the adviser to describe so you easily understand.
- The adviser promotes benefits like exclusivity, which don't impact performance.
- You didn't do your own due diligence, but a trusted intermediary did.

This was Sir Allen Stanford's game—as well as scores of other scamsters in history. He sold (fake) CDs guaranteeing 14% and 15% yields (or more) when comparable (but real) CDs were paying closer to 2% and 3%. His investors learned the hard way those returns were indeed too good to be true.

This is why it's critical you correctly assess what your return expectations are. You don't want to find yourself in a situation where you can be tempted by huge (but possibly false) returns to make up for lost opportunity. If that's where you are, better to adjust your goals (downgrade your long-term return expectations and/or cash flow needs) than get involved in what seems like a "can't lose" investment with pie-in-the-sky return promises. Because if you've suffered opportunity cost over a long time period, you really don't want to suffer the potential total loss of a financial scam.

Recap

Return expectations, a key determinant of a proper benchmark, link directly to your growth goal but also your cash flow goal.

In determining your return expectations, it's critical you don't underestimate your growth needs. But it's also critical you don't set unreasonable expectations—that can set you up for taking on more volatility than is necessary. At worst, it can increase the odds you fall prey to a financial scammer.

When thinking about return expectations, consider:

- What is a reasonable return over your time horizon ahead, and what degree of volatility should you expect to achieve that return?
- What degree of growth are you targeting? Is keeping pace with inflation enough, or do you need something closer to market-like returns?
- Don't forget to consider your cash flow goal. Relative to your cash flow goal, what's more important? Growth? Cash flow? Is one much more important than the other? Are they equally important?'

CHAPTER **6**

Getting That Cash Flow

Next up in determining the right benchmark: cash flow needs.

A common statement folks make about their investments is "I need this to provide for me in retirement." They want their portfolio to kick off enough cash to cover living expenses—now or in the future, partially or wholly. Maybe those are *your* living expenses (when I say "your" I'm including your spouse, if you have one). Maybe they're yours and/or living expenses of a loved one—a parent, a child still living with you.

But how much do you need? Many investors—even those about to retire, even those *already retired*—may not know. And if they do know, they may not know if that amount is feasible now and for the rest of their time horizon (provided they're even thinking about time horizon right).

Then, too, plenty of mythology abounds about how to get income from a portfolio and what a reliable level of income is. This chapter covers:

- Why a portfolio full of high-dividend stocks won't guarantee secure future cash flows
- Why "income" and "cash flow" aren't necessarily the same thing
- How to project future cash flow needs
- Ways to determine if your desired cash flow level is reasonable and feasible

Potential Pitfall: The All High-Dividend Portfolio

But first, an important pitfall to avoid.

A piece of advice you might commonly hear or read is the best way to ensure retirement income is a heavy allocation of high dividend-yielding stocks and/or fixed income with high coupon rates.

First, this confuses *income* with *cash flow*. Dividends and coupon payments are indeed considered *income*—you report them as such on your tax returns. Nothing wrong with these two sources of cash flow. But if you rely on them *solely*, you could be selling yourself short.

Finance theory is clear: After taxes, you should be agnostic about the source of your cash flow. It doesn't matter whether you get cash flow from dividends, bond interest, or the sale of a security. What's most important is you remain optimally invested based on a benchmark tailored to you. And a portfolio full of high-dividend stocks may not do it. Why?

All major categories of stocks come in and out of favor—including high-dividend stocks. Value and growth trade leadership, as do small cap and big cap. All major sectors rotate, going through periods they lead and periods they lag. This is no different—sometimes high-dividend stocks do really well, and sometimes they do dreadfully.

There's nothing inherently better about a firm that pays a dividend; it's just a different way of generating shareholder value. For example, if a firm can generate more shareholder value by reinvesting profits, it may choose to do so rather than paying a dividend. If a firm decides reinvestment won't yield much additional growth (either because of where it is in a market cycle or because of the nature of the firm's business or some other reason), shareholder value can be generated through paying dividends. For this reason, there is some overlap in high-dividend categories and value, whereas growthier firms tend to pay low or no dividends (generally—this isn't a hard-and-fast rule).

You see this as a shareholder. When a firm pays a dividend, the share price *falls* by about the amount of the dividend, all else being equal. After all, the firm is giving away a valuable asset—cash.

And there's nothing about dividend-paying firms that makes them inherently better. Plenty of investors believe value is superior to growth (and vice versa), big to small (and the reverse), this to that, high-dividends to nondividends. But that isn't so. To believe any one category is inherently superior is to disavow basic tenets of capitalism.

What's more, dividends *aren't guaranteed.* Firms that pay them can and do (and will) cut the dividend—or axe it altogether. PG&E, a utility with a long history of paying dividends, stopped for four years while its stock fell from the low $30s to around $5 between 2001 and 2002. Banks (and plenty of other firms) slashed their dividends during the 2008 credit crisis. It isn't even just during crises: GE cut its dividend due to unique struggles in 2018. Through early November 2024, five publicly traded real estate investment trusts (REITs)—frequent targets for dividend-focused investors—suspended payouts altogether. Another six cut theirs.[1]

Folks also tend to think the existence of a dividend says something about a firm's health. After all, a firm must be awash in cash to pay a dividend, right? While PG&E experienced its aforementioned price fall, its dividend yield *rose*—because dividend yield is a function of past payments and current stock prices. A higher yield was just a symptom of a falling stock price (and then PG&E suspended the dividend altogether). And now-defunct Lehman Brothers paid a dividend in August 2008—just weeks before imploding. Dividends don't signal sure safety.

What about bond interest? If you rely wholly or partially on interest from bonds, you might end up with a too-large fixed-income allocation that isn't optimal for you, which could impact the likelihood you achieve your goals over the long term.

Then, you can't forget about reinvestment risk. Sure, as I write now in late 2024, you can buy a 10-year Treasury bond yielding a snazzy 4.5%. But are you sure you can find a similarly yielding replacement with a similar level of risk when it matures in 2034? Bond yields aren't carved in stone. They can and do fluctuate. What if yields are lower a decade from now and you can't find high-quality bonds to replace all the income you are about to lose? What if you have to venture into junk-rated bonds, which may not match your need or desire for less expected volatility?

This is a real-world problem, not theoretical. Rewind and put yourself in the shoes of someone who had a 10-year bond paying a 5% coupon maturing in 2012. What would have then been a recently issued bond, similar in all ways—term, risk profile, etc.—yielded just 1.5%. US Treasury yields stayed abysmally low most of the 2010s. Even junk bonds didn't pay much! To get anything near what you had grown used to, you would have had to venture into some extremely dodgy markets, where repayment of your principal would have seemed far from a sure thing.

Maybe bond yields rise from here. That would solve reinvestment risk, but there is a tradeoff: Interest-rate risk. When bond yields rise, bond prices drop, eroding the value of the bonds you hold now. That might not matter to you if you plan to hold to maturity. But what if you have a sudden need for cash and have to sell securities? You could take steep losses on bonds you have to sell if rates are above where you bought them. Many investors unfortunately saw this very thing in 2022.

There's nothing wrong with getting cash flow from dividends or bonds, but you shouldn't assume they're risk free. And you shouldn't be shackled to them only.

Homegrown Dividends

The most important factor for long-term success in retirement investing planning, in my view, is picking and sticking to a wise benchmark. A rigid allocation to high-dividend stocks and/or bonds just for the income may not be consistent with your benchmark. So how can investors get retirement cash flow?

Through *homegrown dividends*. The term is mine—it means harvesting your portfolio, however appropriate, for cash.

And to do that, you can sell securities. You can! Folks often say, "But I don't want to sell principal!" Why not? That's what it's there for. Plus, buying and selling individual securities is incredibly cheap—there's little impediment to keeping your portfolio optimally invested based on your benchmark and selling securities now and then to raise cash.

And you'll likely still have some cash flow from dividends—a well-diversified portfolio will likely always include some dividend-paying stocks. But you needn't be hamstrung by just those with higher yields. And depending on your goals and time horizon, you may have some bonds kicking off coupon payments—but depending on your benchmark, that may not be a requirement.

In creating a retirement investing plan, you should care much more about *total return*—i.e., price appreciation plus dividends/interest—rather than just yield. That allows you to pick a benchmark based on your goals and time horizon, not just on a dividend yield. Focusing solely on dividend yield can mean badly lagging what you would have gotten otherwise as high-dividend stocks go out of favor or watching dividends periodically shrink or get cut. Not a great strategy.

How Much Do You Need?

Next, consider how much you need in cash flow—now or in the future. Do you even know?

This book isn't about budgeting, and there are plenty of personal finance books that can help you there, as well as common software tools. Some people do a monthly budget; others do an annual one. I have no view on which is better—it's your personal preference, and you should do whatever makes the most sense to you. If it makes sense to you, you'll be more likely to do it and stick with it.

Then, too, if you're already in retirement, you'll have a better idea of what your expenses are and will be. If you're a ways out, you'll need to make some projections, which is fine—just be sure to be thorough and reasonable. If you aren't confident it's right, go back until you are. No book can do this for you—this requires homework by you and is totally personal to your household. But it's critical. If you don't know what your expenses are or will be, you can't know if the cash flow your portfolio kicks off is or will be sufficient. And there's no way to know what an optimal benchmark is.

There are "rules of thumb" about how to project retirement income needs. I'm never a fan of rules of thumb, so be skeptical about using any projecting cash flow needs (and, heck, anything at all). Some suggest you should take your current income needs and assume you'll need 70% to 80% in retirement. The idea is that in retirement you aren't caring for kids, buying pricey work clothes, etc. Maybe the house is paid off. You slow down a bit—so goes the mythology.

Except I don't buy any of that. Retirees I know—many of them—say they're *busier* after they retire. They join clubs. They have hobbies. Maybe they're on a board or two. They travel. They spoil the grandkids. It isn't necessarily a snoozy time spent dozing in a hammock.

As with any rule of thumb, the 70% rule ignores your personal situation, and you don't want to discover a few years into retirement you need much more but just didn't plan for it.

In Appendix B, I provide a basic list you can use (or add to or amend as you choose) to help you think about what your income is and what your expenses are or will be.

If you've never done this exercise before—stop. Go no further (or at least, go no further than the end of this chapter), and figure out what your likely expenses are. And in Appendix C, I provide a more detailed list of common expense categories, if you care to get more exhaustive. Also, don't forget to adjust for future inflation. (We get into that in Chapter 7.)

It's also important to know what's a basic expense versus discretionary—but even that is a bit subject to your personal situation and preferences. Maybe you see yard care as discretionary—make it drought-friendly and be done!—but SoulCycle as non-negotiable. You may view cable as discretionary but golf as a required, vital expense. I don't golf—not my thing. My hobby is redwoods, and walking around redwood forests is very cheap. But I couldn't live without it, so, in my case, sturdy walking shoes are a basic expense, not discretionary. You get the idea.

Then, make a list of likely income sources (again, see Appendix B). Will you get pension income? If so, how likely is that to be there when you retire? Will you have rental income? Income from ownership in a business? What about Social Security? Compare your expenses to your income—the gap is what you should plan for your portfolio to cover.

Count on Social Security—Yes or No?

Many posit Social Security will be bankrupt before they can collect. Whether it will be or not I can't predict.

Social Security is a legislated entitlement that can change—or go poof—with a simple vote of politicians. My sense is if the official accounting for Social Security starts looking especially egregious, Congress will just change the rules for how they account for it (yet again—they've already done it many times). And if it becomes truly unsustainable (which, in my view, will take politicians many years, if not decades, to admit—they don't want to annoy retirees and soon-to-be retirees who vote heavily), yes, it may go away. Maybe it gets replaced with something else. Maybe not.

All this is likely a ways off, and it does no good to make projections on things that will be decided by future politicians and their future motives—which are inherently unknowable. And if you try to guess what a politician is thinking, you may end up in need of medical attention from a mental professional.

If you're younger and particularly worried you won't collect, the answer is easy—don't count on it. Know you must make up for that income another way, and start planning now. If you do end up collecting, consider it gravy. If you consider paying taxes now for an entitlement you may never collect later an injustice, well, consider this a valuable lesson learned early on how politicians operate.

But once you know how much you need, you aren't done. Why?

You must consider how important the cash flow goal is relative to other goals. That may seem silly—if you need cash flow, you need cash flow, right?

Yes, except, as with the growth goal, there may be magnitudes here. Some considerations:

- What will the cash flow be used for? Basic living expenses? Discretionary expenses? Some combination?
- When do you need the cash flow?
- Is your focus almost exclusively on cash flow, never mind the value of the portfolio?
- Is your focus mostly cash flow, but you do likely need the portfolio to stretch some (whether a lot or a little) to cover inflation-adjusted distributions over your time horizon?
- If your cash flows are discretionary, is your cash flow about as equal a goal as growth?
- Is cash flow a goal but growth much more important? For example, when your portfolio's value is down on a near-term basis (as will happen), are your cash flow needs rigid? Or can you delay some discretionary spending?
- Do you want the value of your portfolio to grow over time (on average), even though you're taking some cash flow?

These are just a few scenarios—the idea is to understand your cash flow goal in the context of your growth goal (if you have or require one). And keep in mind, this can change! Hence, you should revisit your goals about once a year to make sure your benchmark is still optimal.

You may like the final scenario—growing your portfolio while taking cash flow. Who wouldn't want that? But remember, if you have big cash flow needs, that likely becomes tough to do. As said earlier, if you require 20% of your portfolio each year and expect the portfolio to grow above and beyond that, your expectations are likely way out of whack.

The 10% Myth

A frequent refrain I have encountered is, since markets return about 10% a year, you can safely take that much in cash flow annually. Just skim off the top, so to speak.

But this ignores the huge variability of returns. As discussed in Chapter 5, stocks rarely return about 10% a year. Yes, they often return much more! But they also can return much less. If you take 10% in a year stocks are down 20%, 30%, or more, you've put yourself in a bigger hole, making it that much harder for your portfolio to recover.

Now, some may say, "That's fine—I just won't have such a volatile portfolio that's down 30%." Fair enough! To do that, you need more fixed income, and your future long-term returns likely won't average 10% annually.

A variation on this theme is that folks may say, "I'll just take the gains." Years stocks are up 30%—woo-hoo, party time! Take the gain. Taxes reduce your net take, but you still get a tidy income.

But what do you do years when stocks are down? If stocks fall 22%, do you just not take any cash flow? Or do you *add* cash to get the portfolio back to the arbitrary break-even point again? And then, when do you start taking cash flow again? Say you start with a $1 million portfolio (good for you). First year, it falls 20%. Now you have $800,000. Do you wait to take cash flow again when the portfolio breaches the $1 million level? (Theoretically, it shouldn't take long, since early bull market returns are often huge.) But that can mean going some time without cash flow. Many people can't live with (or don't want to live with) that much income variability.

The goal should be to plan for a cash flow goal that's no more variable than you can handle that also allows you to achieve the totality of your goals.

Monte Carlo: Not Just a Casino

But how can you know if your cash flow goal is reasonable? A good tool professionals often use is a *Monte Carlo simulation.* A Monte Carlo simulation approximates the probability of certain outcomes using random variables run in multiple iterations.

For example, let's say you want to calculate the odds of flipping five coins simultaneously, all landing on tails. The random variable here is heads versus tails. In the simulation, five coins would be flipped to see if all five came up tails. The analysis would run this over and over (multiple iterations) and report the results—i.e., how many times all five landed on tails, what the biggest winning and losing streaks on average were, how many times in a row you could get five tails, etc. The more iterations run, the better and more scientific the findings.

You can build your own Monte Carlo simulation—Excel makes it (relatively) easy for you, plus you can buy plug-ins to make it easier. A basic Internet search ("Monte Carlo Excel") should yield plenty of help—or any college student who has taken statistics can probably help you. The hardest part will probably be getting the data. You can find free market data from a variety of finance websites—you just want to make sure you have enough data going back far enough. For folks wanting a Monte Carlo simulation but not wanting to build one, it may be easier to work with a professional to create one.

Or you can find one online (there's one here: www.money chimp.com/articles/volatility/montecarlo.htm). They'll typically ask you to input assumptions, like expected rate of return, expected standard deviation (i.e., volatility), how much you're starting with, how much you're adding annually, when you'll begin withdrawing money, and how much you plan on withdrawing. Note, you should look into how many iterations they run and which data they're using. (Are they weekly data? Monthly? How far back? Total return or price level?) A free online service probably won't be terrifically robust, but it's likely better than doing no simulation at all, so long as you take the results with many grains of salt.

Let's Get Simulating

Your goal with a Monte Carlo is producing probabilities based on a set of assumptions—starting portfolio value, cash flow levels, and time horizon. To give you a general idea, the following scenarios (Tables 6.1–6.4) show the impact of differing inflation-adjusted cash flows on a hypothetical $1 million portfolio.

In each, three different portfolio allocations (i.e., benchmarks) were used—50% stocks/50% bonds, 70% stocks/30% bonds, and 100% stocks. We measured the "probability of an ending balance greater than 0," i.e., whether the portfolio was worth anything after 30 years. Think of that as general portfolio survival (i.e., does the portfolio totally deplete or not).

We also measured "probability of an ending balance greater than $1 million"—which is self-explanatory.

"Worst-observed survival" is the number of years the portfolio lasted, stringing together a series of worst-case–scenario monthly and annual historical returns. "Average years survived" is also self-explanatory, and "median terminal value" is the dead middle portfolio value of all the simulations after 30 years.

Table 6.1 Scenario 1: $100,000 from $1 Million (10%)

10%–$100,000 off $1,000,000–30 Year TH

Asset Allocation–100%

Stats	Terminal Value ($)	Nominal Annual Avg. Returns (%)	Survived Years
Median	$0.00	7.97%	15.08
Average	$3,44,532.18	7.57%	17.45
Std. Dev.	$11,33,599.42	3.88%	7.19
Minimum	$0.00	-4.40%	7.17

Probability of Ending Balance > $1,000,000 : 9.48%

Probability of Survival (Min. Threshold = $0) : 15.22%

Asset Allocation–70%/30%

Stats	Terminal Value ($)	Nominal Annual Avg. Returns (%)	Survived Years
Median	$0.00	7.23%	13.83
Average	$10,036.06	6.91%	15.14
Std. Dev.	$72,987.11	2.79%	5.03
Minimum	$0.00	-1.42%	8.08

Probability of Ending Balance > $1,000,000 : 0.00%

Probability of Survival (Min. Threshold = $0) : 2.85%

Asset Allocation–50%/50%

Stats	Terminal Value ($)	Nominal Annual Avg. Returns (%)	Survived Years
Median	$0.00	6.63%	13.08
Average	$0.00	6.43%	13.64
Std. Dev.	$0.00	2.18%	2.92
Minimum	$0.00	0.27%	8.75

Probability of Ending Balance > $1,000,000 : 0.00%

Probability of Survival (Min. Threshold = $0) : 0.00%

Monte Carlo simulation is a nonlinear statistical method and allows for the assignment of probabilities to various outcomes. All values are expressed in today's dollars.
Source: FactSet and Finaeon, Inc., as of 10/17/2024. S&P 500 Total Return Index, US 10-Year Government Bond Index, Consumer Price Index, 12/31/1925 – 12/31/2023.

These simulations as they appear here are not recommendations because, of course, this being a book, we can't know the totality of your goals and circumstances. Nor are they projections or forecasts. The median terminal value is literally the median of the iterations—half came in below, half above. Rather, these simulations are meant to demonstrate how to consider probabilities. A Monte Carlo simulation can help you (or you and your professional) consider probabilities a benchmark strategy can sustain a level of cash flow for your time horizon. It can also aid in helping you understand risk and return characteristics of a specific benchmark. In that way, it can help shape forward-looking expectations. But it does not supplant the deliberate process of considering time horizon, return expectations, cash flow needs and your current situation, circumstances, and comfort level with the market's ups and downs in determining a benchmark.

We ran 2,500 iterations on approximately 100 years of monthly market and inflation data—sufficient in my view to make a meaningful observation. More iterations wouldn't necessarily result in more clarity. I also used the S&P 500 as a proxy for stocks. Investing globally is better for most, but we have excellent data going back longer for US stocks. Plus, the US stock market is and has been sufficiently broad to serve as a good global proxy when making historical observations.

Table 6.1 shows the hypothetical results of an investor taking annual $100,000 inflation-adjusted withdrawals from that $1 million starting-value portfolio over 30 years. Here, the survival probability is very low across all allocations. The 100% stock allocation was best at 15.22%—but still low.

Worst-observed survival years are also low for all. (Again, these are the very worst of all 2,500 iterations—effectively stringing together history's worst months one after another, regardless of when they actually occurred.) It's worst for the 100% stock allocation at just 7.17 years, and best but still low for 50/50 at 8.75 years. Average years survived is best for 100% stocks at 17.45 years—but still far shy of the 30-year period. And median terminal values for all are $0.

That doesn't mean the weird and wacky can't happen in the future! A Monte Carlo simulation is no guarantee—good or bad. However, this tells you portfolio-survival probabilities with cash flows this high are very low. If your plan is to start with a 10% distribution and not alter that inflation-adjusted dollar amount at all for 30 years (or more), you might want to rethink some things.

Also remember, this is showing a long time horizon. A shorter time horizon of 5 or 10 years would have different results. But since most readers of this book likely have a longer time horizon, 30 years seems sufficient to demonstrate the Monte Carlo tool.

Table 6.2 simulates taking annual inflation-adjusted withdrawals of $70,000 from a $1 million starting-value portfolio over 30 years.

Probabilities for portfolio survival improve materially when taking smaller distributions over a longer period—but still aren't great in this scenario. The 100% stock allocation survival probability is best but still not terrific at 52.33%. Worst-observed and average years survived improve here—average years survived for all scenarios are relatively similar. Median terminal values for 50/50 and 70/30 are both $0, and the 100% median terminal value is a fairly low $133,901.

If you have a 30-year time horizon and plan on a similar level of withdrawals, be aware of the high probability the portfolio runs down materially. Maybe that's okay with you! Maybe it isn't and you want to consider reducing your living expenses. Or if you aren't close to retirement yet, you know you may need a bigger starting value—reducing the relative size of the withdrawals. Or maybe you need another source of retirement income—from a pension (if you have it), rental income, your spouse's income, etc.

Table 6.2 Scenario 2: $70,000 from $1 Million (7%)

7%–$70,000 off $1,000,000–30 Year TH

Asset Allocation–100%

Stats	Terminal Value ($)	Nominal Annual Avg. Returns (%)	Survived Years
Median	$1,33,900.90	8.49%	30.00
Average	$15,95,100.47	8.08%	25.02
Std. Dev.	$26,37,505.60	3.41%	6.27
Minimum	$0.00	−1.77%	10.33

Probability of Ending Balance > $1,000,000 : 37.81%

Probability of Survival (Min. Threshold = $0) : 52.33%

Asset Allocation–70%/30%

Stats	Terminal Value ($)	Nominal Annual Avg. Returns (%)	Survived Years
Median	$0.00	7.43%	25.33
Average	$4,91,880.32	7.24%	24.29
Std. Dev.	$9,25,673.48	2.35%	5.77
Minimum	$0.00	0.34%	11.58

Probability of Ending Balance > $1,000,000 : 18.60%

Probability of Survival (Min. Threshold = $0) : 39.13%

Asset Allocation–50%/50%

Stats	Terminal Value ($)	Nominal Annual Avg. Returns (%)	Survived Years
Median	$0.00	6.66%	22.42
Average	$1,35,503.75	6.52%	22.91
Std. Dev.	$3,41,981.57	1.81%	5.34
Minimum	$0.00	0.82%	12.58

Probability of Ending Balance > $1,000,000 : 4.82%

Probability of Survival (Min. Threshold = $0) : 22.43%

Monte Carlo simulation is a nonlinear statistical method and allows for the assignment of probabilities to various outcomes. All values are expressed in today's dollars.
Source: FactSet and Finaeon, Inc., as of 10/17/2024. S&P 500 Total Return Index, US 10-Year Government Bond Index, Consumer Price Index, 12/31/1925 – 12/31/2023.

Table 6.3 shows the impact of $50,000 inflation-adjusted withdrawals from a $1 million starting-value portfolio. As you would expect, survival probabilities rise. There isn't a huge difference in survival of assets among the three different allocations. Where the allocations do make a bigger difference is on portfolio growth.

A 100% stock portfolio's probability (in this simulation) of ending *above* $1 million is 62.80%, compared to 32.37% for the 50/50 portfolio. And the median terminal value is $1,771,553 compared to $576,573.

However, worst-observed survival years are 14.08 years for a 100% stock portfolio, 17.00 for 70/30, and 19.08 for 50/50. How can 100% stocks have a higher median terminal value but deplete faster? Easy—volatility.

You can get bigger upside with stocks over longer time periods, but you're also more exposed to equity market volatility. So it's time to think back on your cash flow goals relative to your growth goals. If growth is as important or more important, it might be wise to have more equities in your benchmark. And if cash flow is more important—maybe because your cash flow is going toward basic living expenses—it might be better to give up the probability of more growth for lower expected volatility.

Again, there's no cookie-cutter prescription I can give you here. Rather, I hope to give you general guiding principles as you go through this deliberate process. These decisions should be driven by your long-term goals and personal situation ... and many discussions with your spouse.

Table 6.4 shows the impact of $30,000 inflation-adjusted withdrawals. Across the board, survivability jumps materially, as does the probability the ending value (after 30 years) is higher than the starting value (inflation-adjusted). Again, in this situation, the differentiating feature is the growth goal. Median terminal value for a 100% stock portfolio is nearly $3.7 million, over $2.5 million for 70/30, and over $1.8 million for 50/50.

Table 6.3 Scenario 3: $50,000 from $1 Million (5%)

5%–$50,000 off $1,000,000–30 Year TH

Asset Allocation-100%				Asset Allocation-70%/30%				Asset Allocation-50%/50%			
Stats	Terminal Value ($)	Nominal Annual Avg. Returns (%)	Survived Years	Stats	Terminal Value ($)	Nominal Annual Avg. Returns (%)	Survived Years	Stats	Terminal Value ($)	Nominal Annual Avg. Returns (%)	Survived Years
Median	$17,71,552.50	8.74%	30.00	Median	$10,02,005.89	7.65%	30.00	Median	$5,76,573.11	6.78%	30.00
Average	$30,35,873.00	8.52%	28.67	Average	$14,85,250.83	7.53%	29.02	Average	$8,05,949.76	6.74%	28.99
Std. Dev.	$35,41,115.11	3.02%	3.42	Std. Dev.	$15,85,440.69	2.07%	2.57	Std. Dev.	$8,37,262.20	1.52%	2.36
Minimum	$0.00	-0.54%	14.08	Minimum	$0.00	1.51%	17.00	Minimum	$0.00	2.43%	19.08
Probability of Ending Balance > $1,000,000 :	62.80%			Probability of Ending Balance > $1,000,000 :	50.02%			Probability of Ending Balance > $1,000,000 :	32.37%		
Probability of Survival (Min. Threshold = $0) :	83.01%			Probability of Survival (Min. Threshold = $0) :	82.43%			Probability of Survival (Min. Threshold = $0) :	78.68%		

Monte Carlo simulation is a nonlinear statistical method and allows for the assignment of probabilities to various outcomes. All values are expressed in today's dollars.
Source: FactSet and Fingeon. Inc., as of 10/17/2024. S&P 500 Total Return Index, US 10-Year Government Bond Index, Consumer Price Index. 12/31/1925 – 12/31/2023.

Recall that just because a Monte Carlo simulation returns a median value doesn't mean that amount is guaranteed. It's the median—half the ending values are above, half are below. No one can tell you definitively what stocks/bonds/cash/anything else will do in the period ahead. Rather, you must consider what your goals are and what the likeliest path to get you there is. These figures solely help illuminate that.

The aim of a good retirement investing plan—and this book—isn't to give you any guarantees. It's to help you understand and articulate your goals so you can pick a good path—one that increases the odds you actually achieve your goals.

That's one half of it. Just as no one can tell you where stocks/bonds/cash/anything else go in the future, remember, your own behavior is also a question mark. Plenty of investors with the best-laid plans go badly astray because they get overwhelmed by fear and/or greed and make a material change not consistent with their long-term goals. Then they get overwhelmed again. And again. This is why, on average, investors badly lag the markets they benchmark against.

It may not be that their plan was bad—it could be their brains went bad! They didn't like missing out on the big Tech returns in the late 1990s, so they loaded up there—too late. Then they got hammered more than they should have in the 2001–2002 bear market. Then they decided stocks weren't for them, and they never wanted to own them ever again and sold. Then, after missing out on a few bull market years, they went in whole hog again, maybe just in time for the next bear market. Then, they decided, this time, they mean it about stocks—they'll never own them again—and sold out at the bottom of the bear market. Then, they missed the huge historic surge stocks had off the bottom. And on and on, again and again.

This hypothetical investor (whose behavior isn't all that different from many people's) buys high and sells low

Table 6.4 Scenario 4: $30,000 from $1 Million (3%)

3%–$30,000 off $1,000,000–30 Year TH

Asset Allocation-100%

Stats	Terminal Value ($)	Nominal Annual Avg. Returns (%)	Survived Years
Median	$36,92,111.53	8.82%	30.00
Average	$51,87,366.28	8.82%	29.97
Std. Dev.	$47,35,735.65	2.72%	0.34
Minimum	$0.00	1.47%	24.25

Probability of Ending Balance > $1,000,000 : 87.05%

Probability of Survival (Min. Threshold = $0) : 99.09%

Asset Allocation-70%/30%

Stats	Terminal Value ($)	Nominal Annual Avg. Returns (%)	Survived Years
Median	$25,07,945.99	7.72%	30.00
Average	$30,35,859.78	7.70%	30.00
Std. Dev.	$21,34,422.84	1.90%	0.00
Minimum	$1,31,436.92	3.19%	30.00

Probability of Ending Balance > $1,000,000 : 84.74%

Probability of Survival (Min. Threshold = $0) : 99.99%

Asset Allocation-50%/50%

Stats	Terminal Value ($)	Nominal Annual Avg. Returns (%)	Survived Years
Median	$18,44,398.10	6.87%	30.00
Average	$20,92,458.02	6.88%	30.00
Std. Dev.	$12,01,481.11	1.42%	0.00
Minimum	$2,52,167.17	3.47%	30.00

Probability of Ending Balance > $1,000,000 : 82.27%

Probability of Survival (Min. Threshold = $0) : 99.99%

Monte Carlo simulation is a nonlinear statistical method and allows for the assignment of probabilities to various outcomes. All values are expressed in today's dollars.
Source: FactSet and Finaeon, Inc., as of 10/17/2024. S&P 500 Total Return Index, US 10-Year Government Bond Index, Consumer Price Index, 12/31/1925 – 12/31/2023.

again and again, making radical changes driven not by a long-term plan or strategy, but by a near-term reaction to whatever markets just did. He or she may have had a *great* plan—very wise—but didn't follow it. (If you think this is mere anecdotal evidence or theory, again, revisit Chapter 2—on average, investors do in fact lag the performance of the mutual funds they invest in because they in and out too often.)

This is the other value of having a plan—it gives you a road map and should remind you that when you veer off the intended path, you can get very lost. This is also the value a good professional can bring. A professional not only can work with you to determine an optimal benchmark and plan but can be a cool-headed third party who can remind you of the reasons you chose the benchmark and crafted the plan in the first place. You shouldn't toss your plan in the dustbin just because you think the going is better somewhere else (greed) or perfectly normal volatility is uncomfortable in the near term (fear).

One last scenario—for investors without a cash flow goal. Table 6.5 shows the impact of long-term growth using the same three allocations. Survivability and growth probabilities are all excellent, as you probably expect.

The major differences are median terminal values. This simulation is simply meant to show the impact of different return expectations—and the difference a higher level of expected shorter-term volatility can make. Simply, a portfolio with higher expected shorter-term volatility has a much higher probability of superior returns over a long time horizon. In a portfolio with lower expected volatility, odds are, long-term annualized returns are lower. Pretty straightforward.

Table 6.5 Scenario 5: Zero Distributions

0%–$0 off $1,000,000–30 Year TH

	Asset Allocation–100%				Asset Allocation–70%/30%				Asset Allocation–50%/50%		
Stats	Terminal Value ($)	Nominal Annual Avg. Returns (%)	Survived Years	Stats	Terminal Value ($)	Nominal Annual Avg. Returns (%)	Survived Years	Stats	Terminal Value ($)	Nominal Annual Avg. Returns (%)	Survived Years
Median	$62,77,610.37	8.72%	30.00	Median	$47,72,721.84	7.75%	30.00	Median	$36,19,345.50	6.77%	30.00
Average	$80,45,691.09	8.74%	30.00	Average	$54,54,612.14	7.75%	30.00	Average	$39,84,726.05	6.80%	30.00
Std. Dev.	$59,28,835.63	2.63%	0.00	Std. Dev.	$28,91,202.87	1.88%	0.00	Std. Dev.	$16,77,326.92	1.45%	0.00
Minimum	$9,92,601.79	2.27%	30.00	Minimum	$12,54,816.23	3.03%	30.00	Minimum	$12,90,569.15	3.27%	30.00
Probability of Ending Balance > $1,000,000 :			99.96%	Probability of Ending Balance > $1,000,000 :			99.99%	Probability of Ending Balance > $1,000,000 :			99.99%
Probability of Survival (Min. Threshold = $0) :			99.99%	Probability of Survival (Min. Threshold = $0) :			99.99%	Probability of Survival (Min. Threshold = $0) :			99.99%

Monte Carlo simulation is a nonlinear statistical method and allows for the assignment of probabilities to various outcomes. All values are expressed in today's dollars.
Source: FactSet and Finaeon, Inc.. as of 10/17/2024. S&P 500 Total Return Index, US 10-Year Government Bond Index, Consumer Price Index, 12/31/1925 – 12/31/2023.

Recap

Cash flow (along with time horizon and return expectations) is a key determinant of an optimal investing benchmark.

Many folks confuse "income" and "cash flow." However, finance theory is clear: After taxes, investors should be agnostic about the source of their cash flow, be it from dividends, interest, or the sale of securities. What's more, a portfolio of high-dividend stocks doesn't guarantee a stable source of retirement cash flow.

To know the likely level of portfolio cash flow you'll require, tally expenses and subtract any other sources of income (see Appendix B). Remember to adjust for inflation. (See Chapter 7.)

The cash flow goal should be considered alongside and in concert with growth goals. For example, is the cash flow goal more important than the growth goal? Less? Equally important? To what degree? What is the cash flow being used for? Basic living expenses? Discretionary expenses? Both?

Finally, a good tool to assess the probability a portfolio can provide a level of cash flow for the life of the assets is a Monte Carlo simulation.

CHAPTER 7

Can I Get There?

N ow you know some basic concepts behind picking a good benchmark. But how can you better know where you're trying to go? And if you can even get there, based on how much you're saving?

Many investors plod along, socking away a bit each year. But is the socking away sufficient to create a portfolio big enough to kick off needed/desired future cash flow? Or reach growth goals? Or both? And how big should that portfolio even be? The only guarantees in life are death and taxes (and that politicians will say one thing and do another). But you can reduce just a bit of uncertainty by having a portfolio goal and a savings plan. You may not stick to it, but at least you'll know if you're falling short some years and must make it up. Or if you're able to accelerate saving in some years to compensate for some unforeseen trouble in the future. Or ... or ... or ...

In this chapter, we'll cover some easy exercises to help you:

- Figure out where you are now.
- Understand how to adjust today's dollars for the future—by calculating for likely inflation.
- Calculate how big your portfolio should probably be to provide for whatever level of future cash flow you'll want/need.
- Understand how much you should save now and into the future.

How Much Do You Have?

Do you know how much money you have?

This seems like a silly question. But, like the question of income, often folks don't have a great handle on what their true net worth is—liquid or otherwise. It's hard to make good projections about the future if you don't even know your starting point.

Can you rattle off how much you've got stashed? Part of the reason many investors don't have a good handle is they often have multiple accounts. They have IRAs in a few places, a couple of 401(k)s left with old employers, a savings account here, a brokerage account there. Then their spouse has a similar mélange of accounts.

That's one issue. Another is, with so many accounts, folks often don't know how their portfolios are allocated. They may inadvertently be heavy into one security or category and never know because it's sprinkled over 12 accounts, unwittingly exposing them to heightened risk.

If you're the type who carefully logs account balances and positions every month, first, that may not be necessary. Checking in on account balances too often can lead to some cognitive errors. Are you obsessing over your account values this month versus last? And is that causing angst? And is that angst making you want to make changes? Check your account values and know how your accounts are allocated. But folks who hit Refresh on their online brokerage statement screens 3, 4, 10, 27 times a day risk being too myopic. And myopia can cause costly errors—like buying high and selling low in a panic. Or chasing heat in greed, only to get crushed when the hot category turns cold or even lukewarm.

Make Your Own Balance Sheet

Have you ever created your own balance sheet? Tallying up assets and liabilities and calculating net worth, like a corporation? It's a relatively easy exercise—just takes a bit of time. If you aren't confident you know pretty well what you have and how it's invested, collect your next round of monthly statements and fire up Excel (or use pencil and paper, though Excel will be easier). (If you're a pro at personal accounting, feel free to skip this next bit.)

You can make this as simple or as complicated as you like. At the simplest level, just tally up your retirement accounts (IRAs, Roth IRAs, 401(k)s, etc.) and your taxable accounts (savings, brokerage accounts that aren't retirement vehicles). Also tally other investment vehicles or annuities with a cash value.

Even better, figure how you're allocated now—meaning the mix of stocks, bonds, cash, or other securities. Use Excel (or your pencil and paper) to add up the following broad categories for each account:

- Stocks (including exchange-traded funds)
- Stock mutual funds
- Fixed income
- Fixed-income mutual funds
- Cash and cash equivalents (i.e., money market funds, CDs, etc.)
- Whole-life insurance or annuities (the *cash value*, not the face value, death benefit, or income value)
- Cryptocurrencies/commodities
- Other

You can make a table that looks like Table 7.1. And keep it! Update it periodically—maybe once a year or even quarterly. It has a few practical uses. First, you know what you have, which many people don't. Second, you know what you have broken down by tax treatment, which is useful for myriad reasons. One example: If you're at the stage where you're taking withdrawals, you can plan how to do that more efficiently from a tax standpoint, as Appendix E details. Third, you can easily figure your asset allocation, which many people definitely don't have a handle on.

Table 7.1 Hypothetical Liquid Net Worth

	Retirement			Taxable	
	My IRA	Spouse's IRA	My 401 (k)	Joint Account	Category totals
Stocks	$25,000	$0	$165,000	$0	
Stock funds	$60,000	$85,000	$22,000	$137,000	
TOTAL STOCKS	$85,000	$95,000	$187,000	$137,000	$504,000
Fixed Income	$10,000	$0	$0	$ 0	
Fixed Income funds	$0	$0	$36,000	$45,000	
TOTAL FIXED INCOME	$ 10,000	$ 0	$36,000	$45,000	$91,000
CASH & CASH EQUIVALENTS	$5,000	$15,000	$8,000	$40,000	$68,000
ANNUITIES	$0	$0	$0	$0	$0
OTHER	$0	$0	$0	$0	$0
ACCOUNT TOTALS	**$100,000**	**$110,000**	**$231,000**	**$222,000**	
	Total retirement			**Total taxable**	**Grand Total**
	$441,000			**$222,000**	**$663,000**

For this hypothetical couple, their allocation is 76% stocks, 14% bonds, and 10% cash. Is that wise? Don't know! Maybe, maybe not—depends on their time horizon, goals, and circumstances. But at least now it's at their fingertips instead of needing to shuffle endless pieces of paper.

While you're at it, also make a list of nonliquid assets. This would include:

- Primary residence
- Secondary residence
- Commercial properties
- Private business ownership value
- Collectibles
- Private/unlisted investments (e.g., private equity, master limited partnerships, nontraded REITs)

Add anything else you value that isn't easily liquidated—private credit, other hard assets, etc. Go one step further and create a personal balance sheet that also includes liabilities. Appendix D gives you a basic (but not comprehensive) guide for putting one together.

You can use your balance sheet to compare your income to your assets and net worth as a bank would if you're applying for a loan. And it can generally give you a better understanding of your household's fiscal situation. A balance sheet will likely also be helpful to you if you are doing any estate planning or trying to assess whether your insurance coverage is adequate.

A Savings Plan

So how can you know if your current savings rate will increase the chances you get where you need/want to go? Or, if you aren't saving yet (or not saving much), how can you tell how much you *should* save?

If you read Chapter 6 and looked at Appendix B, presumably you have an idea of the cash flow you want in retirement from your portfolio (expenses minus other sources of income). For our purposes, let's make a nice round number assumption—you want $100,000 in today's dollars when you retire in 20 years.

But 20 years' worth of inflation can make a big difference. How can you figure how much you need in future dollars? Easy: Solve for future inflation. You want to know the compounding impact an average inflation rate will have on today's dollars—do that by solving for *future value*.

If you're a whiz on Excel or have a good calculator, you can do this in three seconds with Excel's FV function (or a similar function in your calculator). There are also a bevy of available online investment calculators, including one on my firm's website that could help. (You can find that one at https://www.fisherinvestments.com/en-us/resource-library/

tools-calculators/future-value-calculator.) For you pencil-and-paper types (or for those of you who want to know what the heck the confounded machines are doing for you), you do it thusly:

$$FV = PV \times (1+i)^n$$

FV is, of course, *future value*. *PV* is *present value*—what the amount is today, *i* is the *interest rate*—here assume an average inflation rate—and *n* is the number of years between now and then.

You already know you want $100,000 in today's dollars and plan on retiring in 20 years. For the inflation rate, you could use 3%—roughly inflation's long-term average. The calculation is:

$$\$180,611.12 = \$100,000 \times (1+3\%)^{20}$$

Using these assumptions, you need a portfolio that can kick off about $181,000 in 20 years.

Maybe, after 2022's fast-rising prices, you fear inflation will be higher. Will it? Hard to know. As discussed in Chapter 5, history is a useful guide. But if you can't sleep at night because you think inflation will average 4%, then plan for that.

$$\$219,112.31 = \$100,000 \times (1+4\%)^{20}$$

Under that assumption, you'd need to grow a portfolio that can kick off just over $219,000.

Maybe you're optimistic and you think inflation will be materially *lower* than average. You could do that, though that's risky. It is planning on something that hasn't happened historically over long periods. My view is that generally isn't a good idea—why start off on the wrong foot? My view is using history's long-term inflation average is a reasonable place to start.

Incidentally, this same formula works in calculating long-term impacts of varying rates of return on a portfolio. Say you've got a $500,000 portfolio and you assume a 9% annualized return. In 20 years, your portfolio would be worth just over $2.8 million, calculated thusly:

$$\$2,802,205.38 = \$500,000 \times (1+9\%)^{20}$$

Back to our hypothetical cash flow: If you plan for about $181,000 (inflation-adjusted) withdrawals starting in 20 years, what does that mean in terms of portfolio size?

Depends on how much you're comfortable taking from your portfolio annually. Recall, in Chapter 6, we did Monte Carlo simulations on certain sized distributions. Obviously, a lower percentage annual withdrawal translates into a higher probability your portfolio lasts longer.

Taking just 1% a year from your "starting value" would be very easy on your portfolio. Divide $181,000 by 1% and you get $18.1 million. Getting to $18.1 million isn't impossible, but I'm guessing most readers find that a bit lofty—unless they have a great job or plan to sell a very lucrative business they founded or have a rich old aunt near death who loves them dearly. (It isn't so impossibly lofty—as I will show you, but still.) Instead, let's assume starting with a distribution that's 4% of your future (and hypothetical) portfolio. That would mean a $4.5 million portfolio ($181,000 divided by 4% is just over $4.5 million—but round to $4.5 million for ease).

It's still a good chunk, but perhaps more doable than $18 million. (And again, this is all hypothetical for illustration's sake.) So how much should you save annually to get to $4.5 million? Again, you can ask Excel to do this, use online tools or try:

$$PMT = (i \times FV) / \left([1+i]^n - 1\right)$$

Think of *PMT* like *payment*—what you're paying your portfolio (i.e., saving) each year. *FV* is future value (the $4.5 million you're trying to get to) and n is, again, number of years. You must assume an interest rate return for i. Of course, nothing is guaranteed in investing—the idea is to have reasonable expectations. If you assume a 20% return over the next 20 years and create a saving rate for yourself based on that, you're likely setting yourself up for major disappointment.

For this, let's assume equity-like returns. Long term, stocks return an average annualized 10%, but for the exercise, we use 9%, which perhaps bakes in some costs and seems reasonable enough for a hypothetical 20-year period. (Again, this is average annualized return—this does not assume your portfolio returns 9% each and every year for 20 years, which has never happened and would be darn near miraculous.) So input $4.5 million future value with a 9% annualized return over 20 years:

$$\$87,959.14 = \left(9\% \times \$4.5\,\text{million}\right) / \left(\left[1+9\%\right]^{20} - 1\right)$$

Now you know you likely need to save about $88,000 each year.

Maybe you're less optimistic and think you'll annualize just 6%.

$$\$122,330.51 = \left(6\% \times \$4.5\,\text{million}\right) / \left(\left[1+6\%\right]^{20} - 1\right)$$

Now you must save just over $122,000. A higher rate of return makes a big difference.

Maybe you need a $4.5 million portfolio in 20 years but find saving $88,000 too difficult. You can always start modest and save more later as earnings increase—though remember the power of compounding interest. If you save less than $88,000 now, you'll need to save much more than that later to make up for lost compounding years. Or you may decide to dial back your future expenses. But you have 20 years in this scenario, so you have time to plan.

A higher rate of return helps and so does a longer saving period. Say you're 25 and planning on retiring in 40 years and want $100,000 annually, and you want to start with a 4% cash flow level. First, adjust for inflation:

$$\$242,726.25 = \$100,000 \times (1+3\%)^{40}$$

See the huge difference inflation makes over 40 years? Never, never, never forget inflation's impact. Divide that by 4%, and you get $6,068,156.18.

If $4.5 million seemed like a lot, $6 million may seem unreachable. But look at the difference another 20 years make. Assuming a 9% annualized rate of return over 40 years:

$$\$17,959.37 = (9\% \times \$6,068,156.18) / \left([1+9\%]^{40} - 1\right)$$

Just $18,000, saved annually, starting at age 25 with a good rate of return, can get you $6 million at age 65. Oh, the power and beauty of compounding interest!

Now, for fun, let's assume an average annual 10% (i.e., the stock market's long-term average):

$$\$13,959.37 = (10\% \times \$6,068,156.18) / \left([1+10\%]^{40} - 1\right)$$

Now you must save just $14,000 annually if you simply match what the market has done. Make no mistake—that isn't easy to do. Tactically it is, but emotionally and behaviorally, it's very tough to do long term. But without even maxing out your 401(k) contribution each year and matching the long-term annualized performance of stocks, you can get a $6 million portfolio (hypothetically) in 40 years. Doesn't seem so unattainable, does it?

For more fun, let's say you *do* max out your 401(k) contribution in 2025 (which is $23,500 if you're under 50) and every year thereafter (assuming the limits don't rise ever again, though they likely will). Solve for future value—use Excel or:

$$FV = PMT \times \left([1+i]^{n} / i\right)$$

Assuming 10% annualized returns over the next 40 years:

$$\$10,400,925.06 = \$23,500 \times \left(\left[(1+10\%)^{40} - 1\right] / 10\%\right)$$

If you take 4% of that portfolio, your annual cash flow in 40 years would be nearly $416,000 (about $128,000 in today's dollars).

If your employer matches your contributions 50% (as many employers do), your annual savings jumps to $35,250:

$$\$15,601,387.59 = \$35,250 \times \left(\left[(1+10\%)^{40} - 1\right] / 10\%\right)$$

Now you have a hypothetical $15 million portfolio ... almost that lofty $18 million! And 4% cash flows mean $624,000 annually (about $191,000 in today's dollars), just by maxing out your 401(k) annually for 40 years and matching the market. Save early. Save often.

Let's go back to the original scenario—the 45-year-old retiring at 65 who needs a roughly $4.5 million portfolio to kick off about $181,000 ($100,000 in today's dollars). But now you aren't starting from scratch. Let's say you already have $300,000 saved. How much must you save now to get to that $4.5 million?

First, figure the future value on the current portfolio, again assuming a 9% annual return, using the very first equation I showed you.

$$FV = PV \times (1+i)^{n}$$

$$\$1,681,323.23 = \$300,000 \times (1+9\%)^{20}$$

Your current portfolio, using these assumptions, grows to $1.68 million. Subtract that from $4,515,278.09 for $2,833,954.86. How much must you save to get that over 20 years?

$$PMT = (i \times FV) / \left(\left[1+i\right]^{n} - 1\right)$$

$$\$55{,}393.83 = \left(9\% \times \$4{,}515{,}278.09\right) / \left([1+9\%]^{20} - 1\right)$$

In this scenario, saving just over $55,000 annually at a 9% annualized rate in addition to your $300,000 gets you there. (Assuming 10% annualized rates, that drops to $49,479.79. Assuming less volatility and a lower annualized rate of 6%, now you must save $77,039.81 annually, if you start with a $300,000 portfolio.)

Is it possible inflation is higher or lower than you project? Yes. Is it possible your rate of return is higher or lower? Or your income needs a bit different? Yes and yes. But by doing this exercise, your retirement planning becomes much more a road map and much less a shot in the dark.

And you'll revisit it occasionally. Once a year would be ideal, just to make sure your future (or current) cash flow needs haven't changed or your saving rate is on target, etc. Isn't there enough uncertainty in investing to not know if your current saving rate puts you somewhere in the realm of reasonable for your goals over time?

Recap

To increase the odds you get where you're going, figure out where you are first. Create a personal balance sheet. (See Appendix D.)

If you haven't done it, make some estimates about your future income needs—use Appendix B to determine future expenses and future income sources.

Once you project a future cash flow, use these calculations (or online tools or Excel) to help project what you'll need to save.

Solving for future value based on an assumed interest rate and number of years.

$$FV = PV \times (1+i)^{n}$$

Solving for how much you need to save annually.

$$PMT = (i \times FV) / \left([1+i]^n - 1 \right)$$

Solving for future value based on an assumed savings amount each year.

$$FV = PMT \times \left(\left[(1+i)^n - 1 \right] / i \right)$$

CHAPTER

8

Putting It All Together

By now, you've (hopefully!) read the entire book and understand some key guiding principles for selecting a benchmark that fits your retirement investing plan.

And no, there's no benchmark recommendation in this chapter, either. Sorry—I did warn you. Instead, this chapter pulls together each chapter's high points as a reference to guide you.

I've given you some principles and concepts for selecting a benchmark—you must now use them to determine for yourself what's right without succumbing to rules of thumb that may sound commonsensical but can actually harm you long term. Or you can use this as a guide to improve your communication (and hopefully, the results) with a professional. Your call.

Picking a proper benchmark isn't trivial. It's yours for a good long while, unless something very major changes. That is why I can't give you a cookie-cutter solution. But if you put in the work—or work with a professional who understands the importance of selecting a benchmark to manage against—and if you remain disciplined to a well-constructed plan, you can increase the odds of achieving your long-term goals. You can indeed get the prosperity you plan for.

It isn't easy. It's quite hard! If someone tells you otherwise, they're kidding themselves. But as I've said throughout the book, it isn't hard because it's necessarily very *tactically* hard. It's hard because your brain didn't evolve to do investing easily. And every single day can be a battle against your instinct to cower in fear or greedily chase hot returns—if you let it. Perhaps the biggest benefit of a benchmark is it can aid you in remaining disciplined.

How so? Remember there was a reason you selected that benchmark. It wasn't driven by whim or a magazine survey. It was the result of careful consideration. You chose it (or it was chosen for you or with you by a professional) because it fit you and your goals. So through good times and bad—however tempted you are to stray—remember the benchmark, if chosen carefully and properly, should increase the odds you get where you need to go over time.

Said another way, deviating materially (for reasons other than material changes to your circumstances and goals) may not end up helping and indeed can end up hurting. It might help alleviate some near-term pain—because either downside shorter-term volatility is uncomfortable or you feel you're missing out on gains somewhere else. But that likely matters much less later on if you discover you aren't close to where you planned to be.

So choose wisely and well—then remember how and why you chose, and stay disciplined.

To Benchmark or Not to Benchmark

To increase the likelihood of reaching your retirement investing goals, you need a benchmark. Picking one is critical and the very aim of this book.

A good benchmark *is*:

- A well-constructed index (like the S&P 500, MSCI World Index, MSCI ACWI, a bond index, etc.) or a blended index (70% MSCI World/30% your choice of a bond index with characteristics that match your goals and needs).
- A road map for portfolio construction.

- A measuring stick for performance. In general, if you can perform like a well-chosen benchmark, over time, it should get you where you need to go.
- A way to set reasonable expectations for future performance. If you've selected a benchmark with a long-term history of annualizing 5% returns but your goals require higher returns on average going forward, you're likely starting down the wrong path.
- A way to help you manage risk. The more your portfolio resembles your benchmark, the higher the odds you get similar returns. The more you deviate, the more your returns can deviate—for good *and* bad.
- Effectively, your long-term asset allocation.

A good benchmark is *not*:

- A poorly constructed index, like any price-weighted index (e.g., the popular but very faulty Dow).
- A guarantee of future returns.
- An inflexible framework.

The benchmark is the backbone of your long-term investing strategy. Every decision you make should be relative to it. The first decision is whether you want to be active or passive. (The questions later in this chapter can help you answer that.)

For example, if you decide your benchmark should be 100% equities and you want global exposure (a good idea for equity investors), you could invest everything in an ACWI ETF—then never touch it for the rest of your investing time horizon. Maybe you add to it as long as you're in your earning phase, and then you sell bits of it occasionally in retirement for cash flow. That makes you identical to your benchmark for as long as that benchmark is right for your goals—that's passive investing.

This is tactically easy, but, in my experience, many more investors believe they can do true passive investing than actually do it successfully. Make no mistake, in practice, passive investing can be very, very hard to do. (See Chapter 2 of this book or Chapter 17 of my 2010 book, *Debunkery*.) And if you have a goal of beating the market (i.e., your benchmark), as many investors do, it simply can't be done via passive.

If you decide to do active, you must decide whether you have the time, knowledge, expertise, and/or fortitude to do it yourself or if you want to hire a professional. Then, too, you can decide (or your professional can help you decide or decide for you) when and where and how you want to deviate from your benchmark. (Again, this book isn't about investment strategy tactics. For that, I point you to the update of my 2007 book, *The Only Three Questions That Still Count*, which walks you through a strategy for how to tactically invest relative to a benchmark.)

But you can't choose a benchmark yet, not until you've done the following.

State Your Goals

Your investing goals are key to selecting a benchmark. You should be able to state them simply, though they can cover a wide array of objectives.

At a very high level, most investors' goals fall into one of these broad buckets:

- Growth—of some degree
- Cash flow—of some degree—whether now or at some point in the future
- Some combination of those two
- Capital preservation (which investors often initially think they want but is often wholly off target for investors with longer time horizons)

For the most part, and for most investors, goals shouldn't be any more complicated than that.

What about "capital preservation and growth"? In reality, as discussed in Chapter 2, *capital preservation* and *growth* are two separate and inherently conflicting goals.

To get growth, you must accept some level of near-term volatility risk. True capital preservation requires complete or near absence of volatility risk. If you have a growth goal and implement it well, over a very long period, you likely will have grown your assets and thereby also preserved your capital. But that means experiencing relatively shorter periods of downside volatility—the opposite of a capital preservation goal. Be very wary of any strategy that purports to satisfy both goals at the same time. It can easily be a recipe for disappointment ... or worse.

There are other goals you can accomplish via financial planning, like insurance and estate planning. However, for the most part, you don't want to commingle insurance needs and an investing strategy.

There are some products, like variable annuities, that purport to grow your assets (like an investment) while providing a death benefit (like an insurance contract). However, combining the two often means increasing costs and doing neither well. You are best served, in my view, if you buy insurance (cheaply) for insurance needs and buy securities to meet investing goals.

Know Where You Are

To know which benchmark can increase the odds of achieving your long-term goals, you should know where you're starting from and what your future needs are. To do that, do a few exercises like these:

- Create a personal balance sheet to determine your current net worth. (See Appendix D.) You can also use this to make projections about future net worth.
- Create an income and expense sheet. (See Appendix B.) Use this to make projections about future cash flow needs.

Picking a Sound Benchmark

You can't get a benchmark recommendation from a book. Nor can a book give you a tailored asset allocation recommendation—the book doesn't know you, your situation or goals. It can't possibly. (It's a book.)

However, you can use the concepts and principles provided here to help you determine what's likely right for you or aid in a conversation with a professional.

Remember: *A properly chosen benchmark should help increase the probability of achieving your long-term goals.* An incorrect benchmark might seem like a good idea initially but could set you up for major disappointment down the road.

What's more, in conjunction with determining a benchmark targeted at your goals, it's critical you understand the risk and return characteristics of that specific benchmark so you can understand—and be prepared for—how much shorter-term volatility you're likely to experience. Volatility isn't *bad*—finance theory says to get growth, you must experience volatility. And don't forget, volatility goes both ways—up and down. But shorter-term downside volatility can sometimes be difficult to experience.

If you're working with a professional, an additional benefit they can provide is helping you understand expected risk and return characteristics of a good benchmark. They can also help you remain disciplined when times are tough. As discussed in Chapter 2, failing to stick with a strategy is one major error many investors make, and it can seriously erode portfolio return over time.

What are the driving factors determining a benchmark? Primarily:

- Time horizon
- Return expectations
- Cash flow needs
- Any other circumstances unique to you

Start by determining **time horizon**, which is

- How long you need the assets to work, not how long it is until you retire or you start taking cash flow.
- Frequently, this is your life expectancy. Don't forget to consider the life expectancy of your spouse.
- Assume on the longer side if you and/or your spouse have long-living parents and/or grandparents who are/were active and healthy.

Then, consider your **return expectations**.

- Do you want to keep up with inflation? Or are your growth goals for something more than that—like equity-like returns? What degree of returns are you targeting?
- Your return expectations should be *reasonable* (e.g., historically average or common). Returns that look too good to be true often are.
- Remember, investors often underestimate how much growth is necessary for their goals.

Next, consider if you have **cash flow** needs.

- How much cash flow do you need? And when?
- Will the portfolio cash flow cover basic living expenses? Discretionary expenses? Some combination?
- Project (as best you can) what your portfolio cash flow needs will be. Do this by determining:

  ○ What are sources of income during retirement? (See Appendix B.)
  ○ What are your expenses?
  ○ Don't forget to adjust for inflation.

$$FV = PV \times (1+i)^n$$

But that isn't all—there are **other criteria,** unique to you, that might affect a benchmark decision. Here are some examples:

- Are you a director or otherwise control person of a publicly traded company?
- Do you have heavy allocation in a stock or sector for some reason that you <u>can't</u> (not are reluctant to, actually *can't*) change?
- Are you opposed to certain stocks or sectors for whatever reason?
- Do you understand the risk and return characteristics of a specific benchmark?
- Anything else?

Ignore rules of thumb about age being the primary determinant for asset allocation. Your age figures into your time horizon but ignores your spouse and your potential longevity. This rule of thumb also ignores your return needs, your cash flow needs, and other unique factors. It's much too cookie cutter and assumes all investors of a same age are in the exact same circumstances with identical goals.

At a very high level, the more growth you need—whether to satisfy a growth goal or to ensure your assets stretch enough to cover cash flow needs—the more equities you need in your benchmark. But expected volatility must be weighed against cash flow needs.

A good tool that can help determine probabilities of portfolio survival given different growth assumptions and cash flow levels is a Monte Carlo simulation. You can build one yourself (if you have the data) using Excel, find one online, or ask a professional to do one. Whether you use a free online model or have a professional run simulations, check how the model is constructed. You want it to use ample data going back far enough (preferably 1926—as far back as we currently have good S&P 500 data), and you want to run many iterations for multiple scenarios.

Finding Professional Help

If you've decided creating and managing an investing strategy is beyond your interest or ability and/or you simply don't have the time, choosing the right adviser becomes critical.

There's no boilerplate right answer here, either. Some folks want to make most of the decisions themselves and only need an adviser who can sell them securities. Others want more extensive help. Either way, the following questions can help you better understand the capabilities of the person or firm you're considering hiring. Ask at least the following of anyone you interview:

Since portfolio asset allocation is a critical decision made for my account ...

- Who is responsible for recommending my benchmark (i.e., long-term asset allocation)? You? Another individual at your firm? Does the ultimate responsibility lie with me?
- How frequently is that decision reviewed? Must I request it be reviewed?
- Who is responsible for making or recommending changes to my tactical asset allocation? You? Another individual at your firm? Does the ultimate responsibility lie with me?
- Would my asset class mix change if your market outlook changed?
- Who is responsible for making market forecasts? Do you/they have a demonstrated history of making strategic market calls? Can I review it?
- What do you monitor to forecast likely market/sector/industry direction?
- How do your market/sector/industry forecasts affect your year-to-year asset allocation mix?

Global market leadership has always shifted and will continue to shift over time ...

- How long have you/your firm been investing in non-US markets?
- Who is responsible for making or recommending changes to my portfolio's domestic versus international mix?
- How do you (or your firm) determine when and how much to underweight or overweight the US equity market?
- How do you (or your firm) decide which countries to invest in and which to avoid?
- Who makes these decisions and do they have a demonstrated history of making such decisions?

Static and/or rigid allocations to size, style, sector mix, or other categories can mean missed opportunities and can hamper performance ...

- Does your firm have a preferred or set equity style? Large or small cap? Growth or value? Something else?
- Will the style mix be static, or is it flexible?
- What would make you/your firm recommend a tactical shift in the size, style, and/or sector mix?
- Who is responsible for making size/style/sector decisions or recommendations? Do they have a demonstrated history of making such decisions?

The right manager's interests are fully aligned with mine ...

- Aside from what I pay you directly, what other compensation do you receive? (For example, commissions from insurance products, incentives for selling stocks and bonds from your firm's inventory, spreads on the sales of bonds, etc.)
- Do you have a service structure designed to help me remain disciplined to a well-crafted strategy through both up and down market periods?
- How frequently will I hear from you? Only when I call?

Avoid Being a Fraud Victim

Another key benefit of having a sound strategy and reasonable expectations: It can reduce the odds you become a victim of a financial fraud.

Never assume you're not an attractive mark for a con artist. Technology has only made their "jobs" easier, and even young, very intelligent people have fallen prey—despite societal biases thinking older folks are the only marks. If you have money, whether 100 bucks or $100 million, that's feed fuel for a con artist's game—and they'll do anything to keep a con running. If you have reasonable expectations, a strategy you're disciplined enough to remain with, and aren't motivated to chase pie-in-the-sky (but possibly false) returns, it's very tough for a con artist to swindle you.

As investors, we're often concerned by the return on our money. But ultimately, if you fall for a scam, your loss can be total. Sometimes, the return *of* your money is more important than the return *on* your money. Know the signs of a possible fraud:

- Your adviser also has custody of the assets—the number-one sign to be aware of. In every financial Ponzi I've studied through history, this was the core feature they all had in common.
- Returns are consistently great—seemingly *too good to be true.*
- The investing strategy isn't understandable, is murky, flashy, or "too complicated" for the adviser to explain to you so you easily understand.
- Your adviser promotes benefits, like exclusivity, unrelated to results or your financial health overall.
- You didn't do your own due diligence, but a trusted intermediary did.

Understand what's reasonable to expect, and you can avoid falling into a fraudster's trap.

And You're Off!

This is only the very start of your journey. I hope you use what you've read here to better guide you to a quality benchmark for your retirement investing plan.

Investing is very difficult. If it weren't, there'd be no need for this book, any of the others I've written, or any of the thousands more written over the years by others. The industry wouldn't have spawned countless products, myriad sales and service people, and firms globally that exist solely (or primarily) to service and advise investors. It would be like falling off a bike. Anyone could do it, and they would, and we would probably all be much wealthier.

And even if you have a good plan and a sound strategy, it still isn't easy. Our brains weren't set up to do this well. We're plagued constantly by conflicting cognitive errors. If you find investing difficult, you're normal. If you find it easy, you're kidding yourself. If you can acknowledge investing is hard and counterintuitive and a lifelong battle, you likely have a bit of a leg up over your peers.

But that's why you need a plan. And the earlier you establish one, the better off you can be. Create a good plan and select a proper benchmark—and then invest using that benchmark as a road map—and you remove one major uncertainty from investing. You won't be stabbing in the dark collecting a variety of products and hoping the mix all turns out okay in the end.

So may the wind be at your back, and enjoy the journey to your prosperity.

Appendix A
All Hail the Mighty Dow

*W**hat follows is an updated adaptation of Chapter 23 from my 2010 book,* Debunkery.

I'm consistently surprised at how many investors—even professionals who should know better—obsess over the Dow as if it were indicative of anything. It's all you hear on TV: "The Dow was up XX points. The Dow fell YY points." Who cares? In my entire 50+-year professional career, I have never paid attention to the level of the Dow—I learned as a kid it is a useless long-term indicator because it is far too narrow and, worse, it is "price-weighted." Never pay attention to any price-weighted index.

In short, despite an army of proponents, the Dow is an inherently flawed index that doesn't reflect the reality of US markets, let alone global ones. Why does everyone fixate on it so?

What's So Wrong With the Dow?

The "Dow" is, of course, the sainted Dow Jones Industrial Average, which persists out of tradition, mostly. That its publisher owns *The Wall Street Journal* (among other publications) probably doesn't hurt either.

Let us start with some relatively minor problems. First, the index is 30 stocks. Just 30! Some of those 30 stocks are pretty big, but the index is just 24.8% of the total value of US stocks.[1] And you get some weird concentrations in some sectors. And it is US-only! So is the S&P 500, but at least its 500 stocks are 85.9% of the total value of US stocks.[2] And the stocks included in the Dow can be included or booted out of the index for fairly arbitrary reasons by those who select the list. For example, Coca-Cola is included, but Pepsi-Cola—nearly the same size as Coke—isn't. Microsoft is in, but Google isn't. Amazon was added ... in early 2024 to replace tiny Walgreens Boots Alliance. Nvidia and Sherwin-Williams are set to join just days from when I type this update. Why? Is it because Nvidia is up massively in the last couple years? No idea. Can't be that they don't want close competitors—Johnson & Johnson and Procter & Gamble are both in. Don't try to puzzle it out—save your brain power for worthier tasks.

Price-Weighted Insanity

Yes, all indexes have their own quirks, but price-weighting is an unforgivable doozy. The only other really famous and widely watched price-weighted index is Japan's Nikkei. (You would do better to track Japan's Tokyo Stock Price Index—the Topix—a vastly better and correctly constructed alternative.)

Price-weighting, despite whatever anyone might tell you, means firms with a higher per-share price impact the overall index's performance more than firms with a lower per-share price. But share price is purely cosmetic. See it this way: As of December 31, 2023, Apple's share price ($192.50) was about one-third UnitedHealth's ($526.50). So UnitedHealth had *three times* the impact on the Dow as Apple—though Apple was (and is still) vastly huger. Its market cap was a whopping $2.81 trillion, compared to UnitedHealth's $487 billion—almost 6:1 in favor of Apple. That's nuts! Any rational person can see that Apple should impact index performance more than UnitedHealth. A firm's share price says nothing about a firm's size or relative importance.

Table A.1 shows all the Dow constituents, ranked by market cap. Note the disconnect between share price and market cap—the actual size of a firm. (You could also do this with the firm's sales, earnings, book value, or whatever and get similar random craziness.)

Here's the real madness of the Dow: If smaller-cap firms with higher share prices do well but giants do poorly, then the Dow does better than the economic return of the companies involved—and by a lot. But that doesn't remotely reflect reality. The reverse is true, too. If those massive firms with smaller share prices do well while the smaller market cap/higher price firms do badly, the Dow does worse than the economic returns of the companies. Crazy!

Better-constructed indexes are size weighted somehow. The most common and most broadly accepted standard (although there are others) is market-cap weighted. In indexes like the S&P 500, the MSCI World Index, the MSCI All-Country World Index (ACWI), the Nasdaq, Japan's Topix, the UK's FTSE, Germany's DAX, and so on—firms that are larger in total market value have a greater impact on index performance—just as they should. Just as a hint, the institutional world (like pension plans, endowments, and foundations) and the professional investing world (like mutual funds, etc.) almost never calculate their performance against anything other than market-cap–weighted indexes. You shouldn't, either.

Stock Splits and Splitting Headaches

Here is where we go into the Twilight Zone. The longer term the results, the more price-weighted indexes are random. Here's why. Splits! In price-weighted indexes, and unlike in the real world, which stocks do and don't have splits actually matters to subsequent performance. Let me show you.

Stock splits happen all the time—but don't change a firm's value or anything of any real worth. Once a firm had 100 shares outstanding for $100 apiece, now it has 200 shares

Appendix A

Table A.1 The Madness of the Dow

Stock	Price (as of 12/31/2023)	Market Cap (Mil USD)
3M Company	109.3	60,379.3
American Express Company	187.3	107,853.0
Amgen Inc.	288.0	154,142.0
Apple Inc.	192.5	2,814,710.0
Boeing Company	260.7	148,232.0
Caterpillar Inc.	295.7	150,834.0
Chevron Corporation	149.2	261,866.0
Cisco Systems, Inc.	50.5	204,633.0
Coca-Cola Company	58.9	229,301.0
Dow, Inc.	54.8	38,464.6
Goldman Sachs Group, Inc.	385.8	125,804.0
Home Depot, Inc.	346.6	346,573.0
Honeywell International Inc.	209.7	138,252.0
Intel Corporation	50.3	211,854.0
International Business Machines Corporation	163.6	149,341.0
Johnson & Johnson	156.7	377,317.0
JPMorgan Chase & Co.	170.1	491,760.0
McDonald's Corporation	296.5	215,071.0
Merck & Co., Inc.	109.0	276,259.0
Microsoft Corporation	376.0	2,794,830.0
NIKE, Inc. Class B	108.6	132,891.0
Procter & Gamble Company	146.5	345,378.0
Salesforce, Inc.	263.1	256,035.0
Travelers Companies, Inc.	190.5	43,507.7
UnitedHealth Group Incorporated	526.5	486,945.0
Verizon Communications Inc.	37.7	158,495.0
Visa Inc. Class A	260.4	414,998.0
Walgreens Boots Alliance, Inc.	26.1	18,722.2
Walmart Inc.	52.5	224,892.0
Walt Disney Company	90.3	165,211.0

Source: FactSet, as of 11/5/2024. All price and market cap data as of 12/31/2023.

at $50—no difference. The total value of the company (simply the shares outstanding times the share price) doesn't budge. But in a price-weighted index, splits have very real impact on how individual stocks affect the index in the future after the splits—because all that matters is the stock price for any given day's return! A stock split halves the firm's future impact on the index—or maybe more, if the firm does a 3-for-1 or 4-for-1 split. (Reverse splits are rarer—but they happen, too, and have the reverse impact.)

About now, Dow proponents are howling indignantly about the "divisor"—a calculation that keeps the series continuous before and after each stock split. And the divisor does that, yes. But it doesn't stop the facts that:

- A split de-weights a stock within the price-weighted index for no real reason.
- Those who like the Dow should have taken a course in index construction.

Here's how you know. We'll do it just like the Dow. Pretend we have a two-stock, price-weighted index with ABC and XYZ stocks. We'll call it the Silly Index. Each has a $100 share price and identical market caps. To get the value of Silly, add the two share prices ($200) and divide by total number of constituents (2) for $100. Straightforward, and just how the Dow does it. Exactly! On day 1, ABC goes up 10% to $110, and XYZ falls 10% to $90—perfectly offsetting. So we add, divide, and still end up with $100. Fine! So far, so good.

Now, pretend both shares are back to $100 on day 2. That night ABC does a 100-for-1 split. That's crazy (so is the Dow), but for illustrative purposes, it's easier to use big numbers because it amplifies what goes on. A shareholder who had 100 shares of ABC at $100 now has 10,000 shares at $1. Either way, he still has $10,000 worth of ABC—nothing changes for him in an economic sense. Nothing.

Not so for the index. Now, to get the index level, we add ABC ($1) to XYZ ($100), divide by 2, and get $50.50. Uh-oh! That can't be right. Nothing changed but the cosmetic share price, but now the index is worth nearly half of what it was before. That won't do. Time for a "divisor"—just exactly like the Dow does. To get back to the correct level, we divide $50.50 by a number that keeps the index level continuous—in this case the divisor is 0.505. Simple algebra to get the divisor.

But it's also weird. See why: Day 3 starts. ABC is $1, XYZ is $100. ABC rises 10% again, and XYZ falls 10%—random volatility perhaps, but perfectly offsetting—just like on day 1. So, add the two ($1.10 plus $90), divide by 2, apply the divisor (0.505), and you get $90.20—not $100.

What? That shouldn't happen. This is the same thing that happened on day 1! If economic reality applied, the index would be $100 again, since nothing economic changed. Yet because one firm split, the overall index level falls nearly 10%. Why? The higher-priced stock fell—and it has outsized impact on the index. The economic reality of the firms hasn't changed, but the index has. If the firms have the same market value, as they do in the Silly Index, they should have equal impact on index performance. They don't. That's the dirty secret of price-weighting.

That's just one stock split. The economic reality of the index gets skewed with every split. In fact, in any year, if the stocks that split do worse than the stocks that don't split, the index does better than the average stock—and thereafter in future years. If the stocks that split do better than those that don't, the index does worse.

It has always been amazing to me how many folks who claim to be professional investors make long-term forecasts about the Dow or talk about its long-term history as if its history had something to do with some real economic phenomenon—which in the case of any price-weighted index is never true. As I documented in *Forbes* columns more than 20 years ago, in a given year, splits in the Dow can throw its return off relative to what the return would have been had those same stocks not split by as much as 10%. And by that I don't mean 10% becomes 11% or 9%; no, I mean 10% becoming 20% or zero. Huge.

We can know two things about those who make long-term forecasts about the Dow. First, they never took a class in index construction—that's a sure bet. Second, they're blowing smoke completely unless they also have some system that somehow forecasts stock splits—and in my life I've never known anyone who's ever even attempted that.

One final way to know the Dow doesn't remotely reflect reality: Very many investors, both amateur and professional, are fond of saying the market went nowhere from 1965 to 1982—17 infamous years of "no return." When they say that, they mean the *Dow* went nowhere. But that's nonsense. Including dividends, the S&P 500 annualized over 7% during that stretch—below average but still positive.[3] Why the huge difference? One, the Dow omits dividends—a big issue, especially the further you go back in time, as dividend yields were overall higher. But also, the S&P 500 is just a better reflection of the reality of the US stock market. Partly because it's correctly calculated—not price-weighted but market-cap weighted—the way indexes are supposed to be.

It's very telling that most new indexes—even those published by Dow Jones—are market-cap weighted. No one really does price-weighting anymore or ever will again, for good reason. We're stuck with the Dow and Nikkei from tradition, and that's a bad reason to stick with anything. Forget the Dow. Your life will be better for it.

Appendix B
Cash Flow vs. Expenses

D o you know what your expenses are? What they will be? And how they stack up against your cash flow—current or projected? This brief guide can get you started. And it's just a guide—feel free to add, amend, blow it up, or use something wholly different. You can also use this to project how much cash flow you'll need your portfolio to provide—now or in the future (Tables B.1 and B.2).

Table B.1 Cash Flows—Current or Projected

Income source	Amount
Salary	$_____
Pension	$_____
Pension survivor benefit	$_____
Social Security	$_____
Business income	$_____
Cash flow from investments	
Portfolio cash flow	$_____
Real estate	$_____
Other	$_____
TOTAL CASH FLOW	**$_____**

Appendix B

Table B.2 Expenses—Current or Projected

Basic Living Expenses	Amount
Housing	
Primary property	$_____
Yard maintenance	$_____
Rental/second/investment property	
Mortgage, insurance, and property insurance	$_____
Home upkeep	$_____
Yard maintenance	$_____
Insurance premiums	
Medical	$_____
Auto	$_____
Life	$_____
Annuities	$_____
Long-term care	$_____
Other	$_____
Car	
Payments	$_____
Gasoline/charging	$_____
Maintenance	$_____
Groceries	$_____
Clothing	
His	$_____
Hers	$_____
Kids	$_____
Utilities	
Natural gas/heating	$_____
Electric	$_____
Landline	$_____
Cell phones	$_____
Fax/Internet service	$_____
Security service	$_____
Health care	
Co-pays	$_____
Medication	$_____
Vision	$_____
Dental	$_____
Taxes	$_____

Appendix B

Basic Living Expenses	Amount
Revolving debt payments	$_____
Total basic	**$_____**
Discretionary	
Entertainment	
Dining out	$_____
Movie/theater	$_____
Streaming/cable TV/subscription services/other	$_____
Hobbies (golf, crafts, etc.)	$_____
Vacations	$_____
Gifts	$_____
Charitable giving	$_____
Total discretionary	**$_____**
TOTAL EXPENSES	**$_____**

Appendix C
Expense Categories

T hough this list is by no means exhaustive, if you want to start building a more detailed budget to help you determine cash flow needs, you can start with these common expenses.

Auto & Transport
Auto insurance
Auto payment
Gas & charging
Parking
Public transportation
Services & parts

Education
Books & supplies
Student loans
Tuition

Food & Drinking
Alcohol & bars
Coffee shops
Fast food
Groceries
Restaurants

Bills & Utilities
Home phone
Internet
Mobile phone
Television
Utilities

Entertainment
Amusement
Arts
Movies & DVDs
Music
Newspapers & magazines
Streaming services

Gifts & Donations
Charity
Gift

Business Services
Advertising
Legal
Office supplies
Printing
Shipping

Fees & Charges
ATM fees
Bank fees
Finance charges
Late fees
Service fees
Trade commissions

Health & Fitness
Dentist
Doctor
Eye care
Gym
Health insurance
Pharmacy
Sports

Home
Home improvements
Home insurance
Home services
Home supplies
Lawn & garden
Mortgage & rent

Personal Care
Hair
Laundry
Spa & massage

Kids
Allowance
Baby supplies
Babysitter & daycare
Child support
Kids' activities
Toys

Pets
Pet food & supplies
Pet grooming
Veterinary

Loans
Loan fees & charges
Loan insurance
Loan interest
Loan payment
Loan principal

Shopping
Books
Clothing
Electronics & software
Hobbies
Sporting goods

Taxes
Federal taxes
Local tax
Property tax
Sales tax
State tax

Travel
Air travel
Hotel
Rental car & taxi

Appendix D
Personal Balance Sheet

Creating a personal balance sheet can be a good exercise to accurately assess your financial health. You can find free templates on the Internet for Excel. Or you can use this as a basic guide. It's just a starting point—feel free to make it as detailed as you like.

A personal balance sheet can be set up just like a corporate one—it lists assets and liabilities, and subtracting liabilities from assets gives you your net worth (Table D.1).

Table D.1 Hypothetical Personal Balance Sheet

Assets		Liabilities	
Cash—checking accounts	$_____	Credit cards	$_____
Cash—savings accounts	$_____	Real estate mortgages	$_____
Certificates of deposit	$_____	Car loans	$_____
Brokerage accounts—taxable (joint, individual)	$_____	Student loans	
Brokerage accounts—retirement (401(k)s, IRAs)	$_____	Personal loans	$_____
Life insurance (surrender value)	$_____	Other loans	$_____
Cars	$_____	Other liabilities	$_____
Other personal property (jewelry, furniture)	$_____		

Appendix D

Assets		Liabilities	
Real estate (market value)	$_____		
Private investments (latest est.)	$_____		
Other liquid assets (crypto, I bonds, etc.)	$_____		
Other illiquid assets (collectibles, etc.)	$_____		
Total Assets	$_____	**Total Liabilities**	$_____
		Net Worth	$_____

Appendix E
Tax-Efficient Retirement
Income Strategies

So you've saved, invested, and built a nice nest egg. Congratulations! Now it's time to start using it. But where do you begin? All investment accounts weren't created equal—particularly in Uncle Sam's eyes. How you sequence your withdrawals can make a big impact on how much of that hard-earned money you actually get to spend or keep.

Withdrawal sequencing isn't a one-size-fits-all approach. What works best for you might be a terrible idea for your neighbor. What works for your neighbor might not work for you—or your cousin, or your sister, or your barber's ex-wife's uncle's former roommate. You will have to get specific counsel from a tax professional to get a plan truly specific to you. But any effective strategy is a personal balancing act that begins with understanding how Uncle Sam taxes various investment accounts:

Taxable Brokerage Accounts	Your standard, nonretirement investment account. Subject to dividend and capital gains taxes—either the long-term or the short-term rate depending on how long you hold the security and whether it is up since purchase.
Pre-Tax Retirement Accounts	Think traditional 401(k)s or IRAs. Money you contribute to these funds isn't taxed until you make withdrawals, at which point it is taxed as ordinary income.
Post-Tax Retirement Accounts	Example: Roth IRAs. Funded with money you've already paid income taxes on. Hence, those using Roths to fund retirement pay no taxes on capital gains or withdrawals.

No Cookie Cutters

A tax-efficient strategy allows you to take distributions you need to live comfortably—and to meet IRS required minimum distributions (RMDs)—while *not bumping you into a higher tax bracket.* Your individual cash flow needs, total income, and account sizes (which determine RMD sizes) will dictate specifics. Hence, cookie-cutter solutions don't, well, cut it. But to get a general sense of the pros and cons of various withdrawal tactics, consider these three general strategies:

Strategy 1: Let Tax-Deferred Accounts Compound

Conventional wisdom holds that you draw from taxable brokerage accounts first and then tap pre-tax retirement accounts like IRAs or 401(k) plans. Leave post-tax accounts like Roth IRAs until last.

Why? When it comes to tax efficiency, brokerage accounts with annually taxable interest, dividends, and capital gains are the worst—so use 'em up first! This lets tax-deferred or tax-free accounts compound as long as possible before Uncle Sam gets his greasy mitts on them.

Strategy 2: Blended Approach

But that conventional wisdom comes with a caveat: IRS-mandated RMDs start at age 73 (rising to 75 in 2033).[1] Let your traditional IRAs or 401(k)s compound until then, and you might get hit with big RMDs you don't need—pushing you into a higher tax bracket in retirement. Not good!

A simple solution: Take distributions from both taxable *and* tax-deferred accounts. This spreads out your IRA withdrawals to avoid a large, concentrated distribution that may push you into a higher tax bracket once RMD time arrives.

Strategy 3: Partial Roth Conversions

Another way to avoid bigger RMDs and higher tax brackets? Shift money from an IRA to a Roth IRA through Roth conversions.

Yes, you will pay taxes on the funds you roll over in the year you make the conversion (at normal income tax rates). So be cognizant of whether that will tip you into a higher tax bracket that year. But the potential short-term tax hit allows more time for tax-free growth, gives you a larger tax-free pool to draw on, and is outside RMD rules. This gives you flexibility to control your taxable income deeper into retirement.

Don't Bust Your Bracket!

A tax-efficient strategy doesn't just vary from person to person—it can vary from year to year *for the same person* depending on your other income sources and needs. Do you and/or your spouse work part-time in retirement? More hours may affect your bracket. Same with one-off windfalls. So be aware of your income as the year progresses. And be aware of current tax brackets, which change annually based on inflation. (See the following table for 2025's.) New brackets are announced each October, providing ample time to prep an annual plan. And watch out for bigger changes associated with tax policy shifts. Staying agile is key!

2025 Federal Tax Rates and Brackets			
Marginal Rate	**Single**	**Married Individuals Filing Joint Returns**	**Heads of Household**
10%	$0 to $11,925	$0 to $23,850	$0 to $17,000
12%	$11,925 to $48,475	$23,850 to $96,950	$17,000 to $64,850
22%	$48,475 to $103,350	$96,950 to $206,700	$64,850 to 103,350
24%	$103,350 to $197,300	$206,700 to $394,600	$103,350 to $197,300
32%	$197,300 to $250,525	$394,600 to $501,050	$197,300 to $250,500
35%	$250,525 to $626,350	$501,050 to $751,600	$250,500 to $626,350
37%	$626,350 or more	$751,600 or more	$626,350 or more

Source: IRS, as of 10/29/2024.

Recap

Tax-efficient strategies vary from person to person depending on individual cash flow needs, total income, account sizes, and tax rates and policies. Moreover, what is tax efficient for you one year may *not* be tax efficient the next. So make sure to regularly reassess several factors:

- Your expected income sources *beyond your withdrawals*
- Capital gains you may realize (and how they are taxed)
- Your current tax bracket
- Other tax policy shifts that could impact you

Once you've done that, you can plan income distributions to target your desired tax bracket. Lather, rinse, and repeat each year.

Notes

Chapter 2 My Goals Are ... What?

1. *Source:* DALBAR, as of 4/10/2024. Quantitative Analysis of Investor Behavior, April 2024.
2. *Source:* FactSet, as of 11/4/2024. Statements based on S&P 500 Total Return Index.
3. *Source:* DALBAR, as of 4/10/2024. Quantitative Analysis of Investor Behavior, April 2024.
4. Ibid.
5. Ibid.
6. Ibid.
7. *Source:* Finaeon, as of 2/23/2024, and FactSet, as of 11/4/2024. USA 10-year Government Bond Total Return Index, 12/31/2021–12/31/2022. S&P 500 Total Return Index, 12/31/2021–12/31/2022.
8. George H. Hemple, *The Postwar Quality of State and Local Debt* (Washington, DC: National Bureau of Economic Research, 1971), www.nber.org/books/hemp71-1, (accessed 6/19/2012).
9. *Source:* Finaeon, as of 2/23/2024. Annualized average of US Consumer Price Index, 1/31/1947–1/31/2024.
10. *Source:* FactSet, as of 11/1/2024. Statement based on US total commercial bank loans and leases in bank credit, 12/31/2022–10/31/2024.
11. *Source:* Center for Financial Stability, as of 11/1/2024. US Divisia M4 including Treasurys, 11/30/2022–1/31/2024.
12. *Source:* Finaeon, as of 2/23/2024. Annualized average of US Consumer Price Index, 1/31/1947–1/31/2024.

Chapter 3 The Secret Code—Asset Allocation or Benchmark?

1. Thomson Reuters, Finaeon, Inc., as of 7/10/2012, Nasdaq price returns, 3/10/2000–10/09/2002, S&P 500 total returns, 3/24/2000–10/09/2002, MSCI World returns with net dividends, 3/27/2000 – 10/09/2002.
2. *Source:* MSCI. The MSCI information may only be used for your internal use, may not be reproduced or redisseminated in any form and

may not be used to create any financial instruments or products or any indices. The MSCI information is provided on an "as is" basis and the user of this information assumes the entire risk of any use made of this information. MSCI, each of its affiliates and each other person involved in or related to compiling, computing or creating any MSCI information (collectively, the "MSCI Parties") expressly disclaims all warranties (including, without limitation, any warranties of originality, accuracy, completeness, timeliness, non-infringement, merchantability and fitness for a particular purpose) with respect to this information. Without limiting any of the foregoing, in no event shall any MSCI Party have any liability for any direct, indirect, special, incidental, punitive, consequential (including, without limitation, lost profits) or any other damages.

3. Ibid.
4. Ibid.
5. *Source:* FactSet, as of 11/4/2024. Statement based on MSCI World Index sector weightings.
6. *Source:* S&P Global, as of 11/5/2024. "S&P Dow Jones Indices and MSCI Announce Revisions to the Global Industry Classification Standard (GICS®) Structure in 2018," 11/15/2017.
7. *Source:* FactSet, as of 11/5/2024. Statement based on MSCI World Index sector weightings on 12/31/2014 and 12/31/2019.

Chapter 4 Time Horizon—Longer Than You Think

1. *Source:* Social Security Administration, as of 11/6/2024. Life Tables for the United States Social Security Area 1900–2100.
2. Ibid.
3. Ibid. Period Life Table, 2021, as used in the 2024 Trustees Report
4. "Paralympic Sprinter Blake Leeper Keeps His Olympic Hopes Alive, but He's in for a Fight," Adam Kilgore, *The Washington Post,* 7/27/2019.
5. "Paralympic Sprinter Blake Leeper's Application to Compete in Tokyo Olympics Denied," Adam Kilgore, *The Washington Post,* 4/26/2021.
6. "A Prosthesis Driven by the Nervous System Helps People With Amputation Walk Naturally," Anne Trafton, *MIT News,* 7/1/2024.

Chapter 5 What's in a Return?

1. *Source:* Finaeon, Inc., as of 2/23/2024. S&P 500 Total Return Index from 1/31/1926 – 12/31/2023.
2. *Source:* Forbes, as of 11/7/2024. The Real-Time Billionaires List.
3. Ibid.
4. *Source:* FactSet, as of 11/8/2024. S&P 500 Total Return Index and MSCI World Index return with net dividends, 12/31/1999–12/31/2009.

5. Finaeon, Inc., as of 11/12/2024.
6. Ibid.
7. *Source:* FactSet, as of 11/8/2024. S&P 500 Total Return Index, 12/31/2009–12/31/2019.
8. *Source:* Finaeon, Inc., as of 2/26/2024. Statement based on S&P 500 total return and USA 10-year Government Bond total return, rolling 20-year periods, 1925–2023.
9. Ibid.
10. Ibid.
11. Ibid.
12. "Chief Executive of Collapsed Crypto Fund HyperVerse Does Not Appear to Exist," Sarah Martin, The Guardian, 1/3/2024.
13. "'I Do Feel Bad About This': Englishman Who Posed as HyperVerse CEO Says Sorry to Investors Who Lost Millions," Sarah Martin, The Guardian, 1/10/2024.
14. *Source:* Securities and Exchange Commission, as of 4/22/2024. "SEC Charges Founder of $1.7 Billion 'HyperFund' Crypto Pyramid Scheme and Top Promoter with Fraud," 1/29/2024.

Chapter 6 Getting That Cash Flow

1. "5 US REITs Suspend Dividends Amid 2024 Cuts," Ronamil Portes, *S&P Global,* 11/5/2024.

APPENDIX A All Hail the Mighty Dow

1. *Source:* FactSet, as of 11/5/2024. Dow Jones Industrial Average total market capitalization as a percentage of Wilshire 5000 total market capitalization, as of 12/31/2023.
2. Ibid. S&P 500 share of Wilshire 5000 total market capitalization, as of 12/31/2023.
3. *Source:* Finaeon, Inc., as of 11/5/2024. Annualized S&P 500 total return, 1965–1982.

APPENDIX E Tax-Efficient Retirement Income Strategies

1. *Source:* Congressional Research Service, as of 10/30/2024. "Required Minimum Distribution (RMD) Rules for Original Owners of Retirement Accounts," 8/29/2024.

About the Authors

KEN FISHER is the Founder and Executive Chairman of Fisher Investments, a $290+ billion (as of September 30, 2024) money management firm serving high–net–worth investors and institutions globally. Ken's prestigious *Forbes* "Portfolio Strategy" column ran monthly for more than 32 years until December 31, 2016, making him the longest continuously running columnist in the magazine's history. He now writes monthly, native-language columns in more than 25 major media organs around the world, including the *New York Post* in the US, the *Daily Telegraph* in the UK, and Canada's *The Globe and Mail*. Ken's 1970s theoretical work pioneered the use of the price-to-sales ratio as an investment analysis tool, and he has authored numerous professional and scholarly articles, including the award-winning "Cognitive Biases in Market Forecasting." Ken is ranked #86 on the 2024 *Forbes* 400 list of Richest Americans and #292 on the 2024 list of Global Billionaires. He has written 10 other books, including national bestsellers *The Only Three Questions That Count, How to Smell a Rat, Debunkery,* and *Markets Never Forget (But People Do)*, all published by Wiley.

LARA HOFFMANS co-authored numerous bestsellers with Ken Fisher, including *The Only Three Questions That Count, How to Smell a Rat,* and *Plan Your Prosperity*. She has also contributed to Forbes.com and other financial publications.

CHRIS CIARMIELLO is a Research Analyst at Fisher Investments. In addition to assisting with books, Chris frequently collaborates with Ken to produce his many worldwide articles. He is a graduate of Connecticut College and The New School and presently resides in Vancouver, Washington.

Index

Index

Index

Index